FRANCE

Steadfast
and Changing

FRANCE
Steadfast and Changing

The Fourth to the Fifth Republic

By RAYMOND ARON

HARVARD UNIVERSITY PRESS
CAMBRIDGE · MASSACHUSETTS · 1960

A people so constant in its fundamental impulses that we can still recognize it in portraits made of it two or three thousand years ago, and at the same time so changeable in its daily thoughts and tastes that it finally becomes an unanticipated spectacle even to itself; thus Frenchmen are often quite as startled as any foreigner at the things they have just done.

Alexis de Tocqueville

PREFACE

On the invitation of the Committee on Regional Studies, and under the patronage of the Samuel L. and Elisabeth Jodidi Fund, I delivered three lectures on the present state of France at Harvard University in October 1957. The directors of Harvard University Press expressed the desire to publish these lectures, which I had given in English without having written them beforehand, and I promised to write the book during the summer of 1958. In the meantime there occurred the events of May 1958, the fall of the Fourth Republic, General de Gaulle's advent to power, and the beginning of the Fifth Republic. A revolution separates the lectures from the book, which was finished early in 1959 while General de Gaulle, elected President of the Republic for a seven-year term, was taking up residence in the Elysée Palace.

It is never easy for contemporaries to grasp the meaning and import of a revolution, even of a peaceful revolution carried out without the shedding of a drop of blood. The observer is afraid of being too severe to the defeated, too indulgent toward the victors, or, on the contrary, should he amazingly enough prefer opposition to conformity, of being too indulgent to those who are on the way out, too severe to the newcomers. He finds it hard to distinguish what has changed from what has remained the same. Is it true that base lead has been transformed into pure gold? Is it true that the nation, divided yesterday, is today entirely united around General de Gaulle?

This essay does not pretend to furnish the categorical answer which only events will supply. The attempt is to carry forward to the end of 1958 the themes of the three lectures at Harvard: the political regime, economic development, the French Union, and France's mission in the world. In the postscript I have tried to interpret the first year of the Republic, 1959.

I am grateful to Professor J. Irwin and Mr. Luigi Einaudi, who have accepted the task of translating the French text into English. Special thanks are due to Mr. Einaudi, who went through the whole translation for a final revision, added some footnotes, and has undertaken to read the proof.

Paris, January 1, 1960

R. A.

CONTENTS

FRANCE

Steadfast
and Changing

The Fourth to the Fifth Republic

I ❖

COMMENTATOR'S COUNTRY

IF the Soviet Union did not exist, France would have the dubious distinction of being the most commented-upon country in the world. Almost every year, some foreigner devotes a book to her, moved, apparently, by the laudable ambition to answer the question: How is it possible to be a Frenchman? Montesquieu had already answered two centuries ago: neither more nor less difficult than to be a Persian. To the imaginary Persian, the France of Louis XV seems no less odd than Montesquieu's Persia must appear to the French reader. But the lesson is never learned and is perhaps destined not to be. If the day ever came when the *other* no longer astonished him, man would probably have lost faith in himself.

It is Montesquieu and he alone who feigns surprise at the ways of the French, whom he knows, and at those of the Persians, whom he imagines. The conversation is fictional and takes place in the mind of one man. Most of the books written by Americans or Swiss on France, at least those which create the image the public will retain in a given year, borrow most of their facts and ideas from French writers. The criticism of France with which such friends of our land reproach a Lüthy or a Schönbrun differs very little, essentially, from our own criticism of ourselves. Self-criticism is, in France, a national sport, if not an endemic disease. Public opinion no more objected twenty-five years ago to the author of *Is God A Frenchman?* than it has to the author of *France Against*

Herself. We get too much pleasure speculating on our decadence or our immortality to hold a grudge against those who come to take part in our investigation, in our unending questioning.

We are neither astonished nor scandalized that foreigners should imitate the French, by whom they are inspired to the extent of espousing the convictions or quarrels of one faction or another. Renan observed it just after the disaster of 1870, and experience multiplies the proof: French politics infects observers with its passions. When the question of France comes up, there is no such thing as an impartial spectator. At the end of the last century Dreyfusards and anti-Dreyfusards were to be found all over the world (there were fewer anti-Dreyfusards abroad than at home). Eighteen years ago a speech by General de Gaulle resulted in the formation of two parties whose voices and invectives were not drowned out by the din of battle. There were Pétainists and Gaullists in French Switzerland and in Canada, in South and North America. In mid-1954 Mendès-France became for a few months something of a world hero. At the moment of this writing, between the Fourth Republic, which no longer exists, and the Fifth, which does not yet exist, the passions of May 1958 are still not quieted, and opinion has not yet chosen the role—gravedigger or savior of democracy—that it will assign to the French premier.

Carried along by the turbulence of our politics, the modern image-makers, the writers or journalists who paint, for the benefit of the crowd, a colorful portrait of the nation, are caught short by events. Less than ten years ago, France was drowsing amid a mediocre prosperity; *Les Halles*[1] in Paris and the houses in ruins were symbols of an out-of-date and stagnant economy. Since 1952 the theorists of French "statism" have observed an unexpected dynamism in industry, inconsistent with the deep-seated trends they were previously proclaiming. But let that pass! For a long time France has been a land of contrasts. We shall add an additional contrast to the foregoing list. A sector of the French economy

---

[1] The overcrowded and antiquated central market in Paris.

(we could take the dominantly state-controlled sector, or that of heavy industry, or of stock companies) may be found in full expansion alongside dormant or undeveloped sectors, Renault among the Poujadists: one more cheap Epinal chromo, close enough to reality to be acceptable to everyone, experts as well as the ignorant. Moreover, the recent expansion of our economy may be reconciled with yesterday's gloomy interpretation by another version of the "technique of contrasts." Since 1953 industry has been advancing at the rate of 10 per cent a year, but it has been our allies, so abused by the nationalists, who have made good the deficit in foreign exchange.

One might give numerous examples of what I have just called the "technique of contrasts." Here are a few chosen at random. In 1950–51 the popular question in the United States was "Will the French fight?" (in case of war). In 1958 the question has become "When will the French stop fighting?" "The sick man of Europe" of 1948 has not regained his health in 1958. In certain respects the disease has become worse, but it is no longer the decline that was suspected ten years ago; it has become a sickness chargeable to the eccentricities of a person in whom new strength is seething. Ten years ago people were wondering whether France was going to drift into communism; today they wonder if she won't drift into fascism (and the two queries are legitimate). Yesterday it was feared that France would die of stagnation. But now observers are afraid she will not stand the stress of growth. Eternal France, whose death is feared at any moment . . .

As for the contrasts that commentators take such pleasure in developing, here are a few examples that might have come from the pens of the specialists: "France is an underdeveloped country, whose railways are the best in the world"; "The French are poor taxpayers, but France is one of the most heavily taxed countries in the world"; "France has some of the finest architects and the most wretched slums in the world"; "The French detest militarism but not war." Finally, one last expression—I make apologies to our

English friends—current in Paris, especially in American circles: "Great Britain is declining in an orderly fashion while France advances in confusion."

These witticisms probably offer us a major reason for the unfailing interest which Frenchmen and foreigners take in the analysis of our fluctuating destinies. In politics, sickness is more interesting than health. Whatever one's opinion of England in the 1950's, the governmental system there has reached a kind of perfection, showing most of the characteristics that the political scientists have decreed favorable to the proper functioning of democratic institutions: the parties agree on fundamentals, that is, on the form of government and the objectives of foreign policy; the alternation in power of the two-party system is accepted by everyone; men's ambitions are directed by the unwritten rules of careers based on merit. It takes many years and proofs of ability in action to rise to the top in a party before becoming Prime Minister. All these statements are characteristic of French politics provided that they can be put negatively. The parties are *not* in agreement on the fundamentals, the alternation of parties in power is *not* accepted, men's ambitions are *not* directed, and anyone, or almost anyone, can aspire to anything, or almost anything.

British politics is full of possibilities for the scientific study of parties, their written constitutions and actual functioning, pressure groups in the House of Commons and outside of it. But how can one get stirred up about this subtle and genteel subject, seeing that the success of one or another entails only insignificant consequences? A game of poker in which one wins or loses beans excites no one. A parliamentary game in which the winner will be named "Gaitsler" or "Butskell,"[2] or even MacMillan and Gaitskell, holds the attention of specialists; it arouses the admiration which accompanies bridge matches played by great players for small sums. Nothing more. The crisis brought on by the Suez expedition suggests that even Great Britain, this perfect example of peaceful and well-ordered

[2] A combination of the names of two ex-Chancellors of the Exchequer, H. Gaitskell and R. A. Butler.

democracy, contains passions which, when continually repressed, give rise to sudden eruptions.

For a generation the political passions of the French have been seldom idle. They are not repressed; they are indecently displayed. One might have said (and often did) during the Fourth Republic that "plus ça change, plus c'est la même chose." Whether the premier was named Ramadier, Bidault, Pleven, Edgar Faure, or Guy Mollet, the change was no greater, and in certain respects less than that brought about in England by the replacement of the Conservatives by the Labour Party (or vice versa). Perhaps it has often been so: a whole theory has been worked out, according to which ministerial crises compromise neither continuity of policy nor stability of administration. Whether true or false, the theory does not do away with the contrast between English politics, exemplary but austere, and French politics, deplorable but entertaining. Government crises, when they were or seemed to be inconsequential, became the expression of the parliamentary game in its pure form, exciting, just as the nomination of candidates for the presidency of the United States is exciting, even when the platforms of the parties are alike. The continuing struggle for positions between parties and individuals contributed both to the defects of the Fourth Republic and to the interest, irritated, worried, or exhausted, with which the world watched it.

Unpredictable in detail, the political game was also often so in vital ways, in its broad outlines. From 1946 to 1948 the Communist Party threatened so-called moderate, middle-of-the-road, third-force governments. From 1948 to 1952 those same governments were jammed in between the Communist Party and the R.P.F.[3] From 1952 to 1954, the breakup of the R.P.F. apparently gave stability to the Fourth Republic. But the problems needing to be solved were formidable both in themselves and for a divided country. And so the last years were marked by a series of theatrical incidents.

Following the defeat at Dien Bien Phu, Mendès-France came to

[3] Rally of the French People, a movement founded by General de Gaulle in 1947.

power in an atmosphere of anxiety, supported by a mixed majority (including both Socialists and members of the R.P.F.). At Geneva he concluded a truce somewhat similar to the one his predecessors would probably have obtained, but he changed its meaning, at least temporarily, by its style. What might have been the lamentable outcome of a hopeless conflict appeared also as the beginning of a national recovery. The rejection of the E.D.C. (European Defense Community) brought on a new crisis which was quickly brought to an end by the French Assembly's approval of the Paris agreements providing for the rearming of Western Germany within the framework of the Atlantic Alliance. From then on, incidents attesting to the unpredictable nature of French politics multiplied.

After the failure of the E.D.C., the plan for the Western European Union seemed dead. Two years later the Rome Treaty creating the Common Market was signed and ratified. The accords on domestic autonomy with Tunisia, prepared by Mendès-France, were approved by the Assembly under the government of Edgar Faure, who, supported by a conservative majority, finally consented to the return of King Mohammed V, and, by the same token, to the independence of Morocco.

When the government under Guy Mollet was formed, the independence of Tunisia had in effect become inevitable. Gaston Defferre drew up the *loi-cadre* providing a sort of domestic autonomy for the African territories south of the Sahara. But at the same time Guy Mollet sent massive reinforcements to put down the nationalist rebellion in Algeria. The chain of events resulting in the fall of the Fourth Republic began with this incident. Morocco and, especially, Tunisia are bases for supplies for the F.L.N. (National Liberation Front). France is both unwilling and unable to use necessary measures against the former protectorates; she would like to close the frontiers completely but she does not succeed in doing so; she could—but is not willing to—strike a mortal blow at these new states by inviting our nationals to leave. Thus France is unable to treat as enemies countries giving aid to the rebels our soldiers are fighting.

These paradoxes were charged to the Fourth Republic; they continue to exist after General de Gaulle's accession to power.

The unpredictable nature of these events, regarded by another observer, might be qualified as incoherence or foolishness. These moody criticisms need not concern us here. These contradictions are one of the causes of the fascination of French politics. The entrance of West Germany into the Atlantic Alliance was approved with near indifference whereas it had been refused with indignation four years before, and the E.D.C. had set off a great historic debate. The conservative government presided over by Edgar Faure, by dint of dodging and false maneuvering, finally agreed (or resigned itself) to the return of Mohammed V. A government under Socialist leadership dispatched to Algeria an army larger and more costly than ever before sent overseas to conquer an empire. But the Socialists had promised during the electoral campaign that the draftees would be brought home.

Perhaps these dramatic events would pass as absurd if commentators did not constantly try to give them at least a theoretical, if not always meaningful, explanation. Frenchmen do not limit themselves to living their politics in an impassioned manner; they comment on them, they analyze them, they elaborate on them, both for their own diversion and for the benefit of others. Literature, along with art, is probably the supreme achievement of the French genius. In France, politics have always been more closely related to literature than in any other country. Adlai Stevenson was surrounded by professors, not by literary men. The Fourth Republic was spurned but also indirectly transformed by writers. Where but in France could the author of *The Desert of Love* have become the champion of the King of Morocco and of Mendès-France? And the author of *The Voices of Silence,* Minister of Culture and spokesman for General de Gaulle?

Since 1945 fashionable literature has been political and popular politics have been literary. "Communism," "existentialism," "engagement"—these words recall to us the main themes of the controversies of the ten years following the war. Even the Catholics have been divided into right and left and have quarreled with an almost unprecedented violence.

A critic would say this turmoil of ideas was sterile and did not influence events. The parliamentary game continued, ritualistic, sordid, opportunistic, while intellectuals gravely discussed the respective merits and demerits of the Soviet Union and the United States, with a tendency to give their verbal approval to the former, on condition that they stay in that part of the planet reserved for the "rotten West." The philosophical discussion, it is true, did not always have much connection with practical politics. But politics was nonetheless affected by the debates on current events, in which ideologies and emotions mingled. For more than three years, the fate of Germany, from the forests where Varus' legions were lost to the Ruhr where atomic bombs will be manufactured, was debated by parliamentarians, professors, and publicists, copiously armed with memories and premonitions, undertaking to demonstrate or disprove the fatality (in both senses of the word) of the rearming of Western Germany. In the case of the French Union, the discussions raise questions about the very principles of national existence. Would France betray her mission by adopting as an objective the integration of Algeria with France? Was France being noble or decadent the day she recognized the independence of Morocco? And what of Madagascar?

It does not appear that the British asked themselves so many questions when they made the historical (*weltgeschichtlich,* as the Germans put it) decision to proclaim the independence of the two Indian states and to transfer sovereignty, at a date set in advance, to the governments formed by the Congress Party and the Arab League. The decision corresponded to the sentiments of a public majority. Political leaders were almost unanimously convinced that no other way was open; necessity, in Great Britain, is accepted as an irresistible argument, not so in France.

The world worried little over the operations of the British in

Malaya against the Communists, or in Kenya against the Mau-Mau. To be sure, those struggles had neither the scope nor the consequences of the conflicts of Indochina or Algeria. Had the British made them the occasion for a major debate, however, the Communists of Malaya and the Mau-Mau would have found more spokesmen in the press and advocates in the United Nations. We French reproach foreigners for meddling in our affairs, but we begin by calling on humanity to witness our quarrels, each of us alleging the purity of his cause and the unworthiness of his adversaries.

This ideological accompaniment to our misfortune is perhaps annoying if only the results are considered, but Frenchmen seem destined never to avoid it. Whatever attitude one assumes toward the Algerian problem, current policy would have a different meaning for foreigners if French public opinion unanimously approved it. The schism of the national conscience is an integral part of the tragedy. The protests against methods of torture do not lessen their horror. One could not understand France if one disregarded either the facts or the moral reactions which they provoke.

The interpretation of events by the theorist and the parliamentarian's opportunism, concealed by able polemicists, give rise inevitably to two kinds of judgments. The famous saying, "No man is a hero to his valet," is still more valid in France than elsewhere. Because our great men have a tendency to set themselves on a pedestal, the analysts are afraid of being duped; some take pleasure in writing monumental histories while others aspire to the clairvoyance of the unbiased observer.

The events of recent years, the Fighting French movement, the liberation of Paris, the fall of the Fourth Republic, the accession to power of General de Gaulle—all offer material as favorable to epic transfiguration as to cynical analysis. Literature of both types is considerable; it helps to keep the reader's curiosity alive. Even the historian most inclined toward exposing guile will not be able to deny the quality of style in the letters of the three Presidents (René Coty, Vincent Auriol, General de Gaulle) during the last days of

May 1958. Of course, it was a question of face-saving for all, of bringing a rapprochement between General de Gaulle and the Assembly, and of creating a seemingly revolutionary situation in which the deputies could vote with clear consciences, not against their inner convictions, but against the opinions they had so often expressed. A Duc de Saint-Simon or a Maurice Barrès would have left us an unforgettable picture of those hundreds of men, stirred by emotions all too human, but the letters of the three Presidents rise to a level where the individuals disappear before the nation's destiny, where historical figures become actors in a drama worthy of posterity. Everyone is free to grant or deny his approval of these texts, written as much for the future as for those to whom they were addressed. No one could honestly be surprised that this drama of political suspense, this literature in action, finds admirers all over the world who are sensitive to the spectacular merits (or faults) which are lacking in both the orderly proceedings of the British parliamentary club and the market-place bargaining in Washington.

Perhaps it should be added that France, whatever the actual influence attributed to her, has been at the forefront of international affairs since 1945. The outcome of the Indochinese war determined the status of southeast Asia, the crisis in North Africa influenced the relations of the West with Islam, the reconciliation with Western Germany was indispensable to the future of Europe. France had the means neither to overcome Asian nationalism, nor to put a stop to the Islamic revolution, nor to organize the defense of Europe. But, depending upon the outcome of her policy, she was successful or not in limiting Communist expansion in Asia, in orienting the Arab-Moslem states toward the West, in bringing the new Germany into the Atlantic Pact.

Once again, then, how can it be astonishing that outsiders are forever studying this sphinx, almost as mysterious as the Russian sphinx because, unlike the latter, she hides nothing and speaks with so many voices?

*   *   *

Experts have distinguished many schools in the literature devoted to the Soviet Union. One might easily find equivalent schools in the literature about France.

A few decades ago a previously unknown type appeared: the expert in "Kremlinology," sometimes called "Kremlinastrology." This specialist undertakes to "decipher" the Soviet press, to grasp the meaning, through seemingly insignificant news bulletins or apparently commonplace phrases, of the vicissitudes of the continuous struggle between individuals or factions. The expert in Soviet astrology foresaw Stalin's death at the time of the doctors' plot, predicted the fall of Beria a few days before anyone else, and announced the conflict between Khrushchev and Malenkov; he knows today the tendencies which divide the Praesidium. This art, which belongs to the same species as the deciphering of codes used by the enemy (or the ally), is based on a few theoretical propositions about the internal structure of the party, the rivalry of individuals, the wording of news items, and so on.

Someone may say that there is nothing comparable in the case of the Fourth Republic; the political battle did not develop there as in the Kremlin, behind closed doors, but in the bright glare of publicity; ministers and deputies talked to journalists in the corridors of the Palais-Bourbon, in the drawing rooms of the Sixteenth Arrondissement and of the embassies. What was there left to read between the lines? The text was not in cipher but written in language understood by everyone. . . And yet a new species of expert in French affairs appeared, concentrating his attention and talent on a strange reality, nicknamed the "jeu politique."

All politics may be interpreted as a game, since all political activity implies the rivalry of individuals and of groups seeking certain privileges, and, even more, the positions from which privileges are distributed. This rivalry, which is no less inseparable from Soviet politics than from American, British, or French politics, is in each country subject to written laws and unwritten rules. These latter are for the most part intuitively known to the players, but they often escape the scholar who looks on from the outside.

The game of politics is democratic when it is peaceable and allows a permanent and legitimate opposition which limits the powers exercised by the governing party. In this respect, the French game was not essentially different from the British or American game. The conditions to be met before a law is promulgated are no less complex in the United States than in France. Nor was it the continuous nature of the game which made the French case peculiar: as soon as the opposition becomes a formal institution, those not in power speak and act with the purpose of hastening the day of their return. The peculiarity of the French parliamentary situation (before May 1958) was the stake in this continuous struggle: the very life of the government was in question at almost each moment, especially during the later years (but the phenomenon, to one degree or another, had been present from the beginning of the Fourth Republic). The selection of a Cabinet was in itself chancy.

The comparison with the Soviet case now becomes understandable. At the Palais-Bourbon, as in the Kremlin, surprises were always possible. The occupants of those two historic buildings all seemed to be performing an esoteric ritual. Here the details of the game were fully known, there they remained wrapped in mystery. But the consequences of too many and of not enough news dispatches were analogous in the long run. Throughout the world the French game seemed incomprehensible, even absurd. There exists a "Bourbonology" comparable, *mutatis mutandis,* to "Kremlinology."

What is the cause and what are the results of this game, obvious and hard to understand in France, obscure and poorly deciphered in the Kremlin? Specialists in the Soviet Union speculate about totalitarianism, ideology, and terror. As for France, what were the realities expressed or concealed behind the parliamentary game? In the Soviet Union a single party, in France executive weakness—are these two facts essential to the Soviet regime and to the Fourth Republic? Is all hope for a change in Russia excluded so long as power there is identical with one party and one doctrine? Was all hope of a renovation in France banished as long as governmental power was paralyzed by internal contradictions? In addition to these analyses of the Kremlin and the Palais-Bourbon, a second definite school, which is always clearly distinguished from the first, insists on the autonomy of the political process. The progress of the Soviet economy would not of itself modify totalitarianism in Moscow any more than the shining prosperity of France in 1957 put an end to the weakness of the government in Paris.

A third school of thought, which we shall link up with the Marxist tradition, tries to explain the political superstructure by the economic substructure. Among the Soviet experts, Isaac Deutscher is the most widely known representative of this school, which is sometimes called neo-Marxist. Totalitarianism, terror, ideological fanaticism have been adjuncts of industrialization, achieved by piti- less methods in a country which skipped the stage of liberal capital- ism. The equivalent in France would be the theory attributed to Mendès-France and his friends. It is the backwardness of the French economy which is the ultimate cause of the political crisis. It is the reform of the economy which, by gradually eliminating out-of-date enterprises or producers, will free government from the pressures exerted on it and from the conflicting interests which lead to stag- nation.

Next in order to the sociologists, the historian comes on stage and invites us to reread either the Marquis de Custine or Alexis de Tocqueville. The Russian political tradition is that of the authori- tarian and bureaucratic state, whose servants, scattered through the provinces, make up the privileged class of the society. After ten months or so in Russia the French Marquis, a reactionary in whom tsarist tyranny aroused indignation, offered formula-lovers an in- exhaustible stock of them: "The kneeling slave dreams of ruling the world"; "Social life in this country is a permanent conspiracy against truth"; "Despotism is never so dangerous as when it claims to be doing good, for then it believes that its most revolting deeds are excused by its intentions."

In France, administrative centralization, a heritage of the mon- archy, has been strengthened by succeeding regimes. Critics, from generation to generation, have obtained facile success by pointing out that the construction of waterworks for the tiniest French village had to await a decision made in the capital. Instability at the summit, it may be added, is less original than sociologists are inclined to believe. During Tocqueville's time, under the July Monarchy, people were already joking about this subject and calling to mind the ambassador who did not know when he left Paris what government he would be representing on arrival at his post. The presence of a king, an emperor, or of a Charles de Gaulle temporarily shields the chief of state from factional quarrels without suppressing them. The chief of state presides at our quarrels; he does not settle them.

At this point we turn to one last school: that of psycho-sociology, of psychoanalysis, or of the study of national character. Why do the Bolsheviks picture the world and direct their action the way they do? Because they follow the rules of conduct developed during the period of revolutionary conspiracy, and their view of history remains that of the Bolshevik sect at the beginning of the century. The confessions which these prosecutors oblige "traitors" to make in public on order from Stalin or Khrushchev reflect this strange system: the "deviationists" inevitably become enemy secret agents, the struggle can end only with the extermination of one of the parties, the individual is always the expression of the historical force, either beneficent or malevolent. And inversely, the dialectic of history is resolved into plots, centers of terrorist action which commit no outrages, in the struggle to the death between the Good (Stalin) and the Wicked (Trotsky).

Through private conversations and outward behavior we perceive a French psyche, of those who participate in the game of politics and those who do not, as typical as the characterization of the Communists even though radically different. Among the performers of yesterday the paradox was the contrast between official pronouncements and true feelings, as disclosed in conversation or confidence. The Bolshevik has deep within himself a belief in his own victory and denies his enemy any right to existence with an intransigence which he conceals. The French parliamentarian never considers conflicts irresolvable, and prepares a compromise even while proclaiming an unalterable will to stick it out to the bitter end. As for the voter, what motive leads him to vote for the Communist Party when he has no desire to join in a demonstration and refuses to take part in a strike whose meaning is entirely political? In May 1958, would the people have accepted the assumption of power by the parachutists as passively as they did the legal investiture of General de Gaulle? *All Gaul is divided;* but to what extent are these divisions real, deep, created by the nation, or provoked by the "system"?

The schools of thought whose tendencies we have briefly sketched vary in theory as well as in method. They consider different aspects of reality rather than suggest inconsistent explanations. For example, the Soviet expert wonders to what extent economic development will affect the totalitarian regime, just as the specialist in French affairs asks himself whether industrialization will change the behavior of voters or deputies. But neither one subscribes necessarily to extreme theory. Economic expansion in Russia, as in France, may be not without influence on political organization, although it may not suffice to disrupt practices frequently rooted in centuries of history and habits which have become almost unconscious.

The listing of these schools requires neither a choice nor a synthesis. The analysis of the Fourth Republic without reference to history would be deprived of an indispensable dimension. The functioning of the parliamentary regime and that of the economy constitute a system even though the connections between them are not always clear.

In each chapter we shall try to profit by the contributions of the expert in "Bourbonology," of the sociologist, of the neo-Marxist, of the historian, and of the psycho-sociologist, without nursing the illusion that we can give an answer to the hardest and most fascinating questions, those having to do with the relations between ministerial instability and economic expansion, between parliamentary mores and national psychology, or between France's past and her present vicissitudes.

The literature on France, the abundance of which discourages one who proposes to add to it, is never at a loss for an explanation. The dispersion of the parties of yesterday is understood, as is the nation-wide rallying of today. By referring to history and psychology, to the social structure and traditions of the country, one makes civil war just as intelligible as popular unanimity. Must we resign ourselves to saying that the social sciences, in the case of France, permit us to predict only the unpredictable nature of French conduct, and to analyse the changes in this unchangeable people, and the steadfastness of this versatile nation?

II ❧

THE SYSTEM

L ET us go back to the beginning of 1956. A National Assembly has just been elected for five years, following the dissolution of the preceding Assembly, whose mandate was to end six months later.

The electoral system was no different from that of 1951, for all attempts to rally a majority for electoral reform had failed. Extremely complex in detail, it may be summarized as follows: a slate or alliance (*apparentement*) of slates obtaining an absolute majority got all the seats from the district; that is, from the *département* (except in the case of the most thickly populated *départements*, which were divided into two or more districts); if there was no absolute majority, seats were distributed proportionally; finally, Paris was subject to a special arrangement which excluded the majority rule.

This electoral law had been conceived by the Assembly elected in 1946 in order to guard against the double threat of the Communists and the *Rassemblement du Peuple Français* (R.P.F.). The preceding law, which had governed the 1946 elections and provided for proportional representation with an extra bonus of seats for the large parties, would have favored those who were called the two extremes, the Communist Party and the R.P.F. So the center parties had agreed, not without difficulty, on an electoral system which would work in favor of candidates who had decided to "ally" (*s'apparenter*), also called candidates of the Third Force. No one, in effect, consented to ally with the Communists, and the R.P.F. refused any alliance with the representatives of the "system" which General de Gaulle had pitilessly criticized. Had the 1946 law governed the 1951 elections, the Communists and Gaullists between them would have held more than half the seats. No government would have been possible without the consent of the R.P.F., which as a result would have controlled the situation. Thanks to the alliances the parties of the Third Force were overrepresented: in more than thirty *départements* they won an absolute majority and obtained all the seats.

The deputies who supported Edgar Faure at the end of 1955 were hoping to repeat the achievement of 1951: that is, to wrest a parliamentary majority from a country which was irremediably divided. They did not succeed for two reasons. Because the R.P.F. had disappeared and with it the immediate threat to the constitutional order, the Socialists and Radicals, on the left, did not enter the alliance and directed their campaign against the parties of the center and the right who had governed together at the end of the session. On the extreme right the slates led by Pierre Poujade won enough votes (close to 15 per cent in the whole country) to prevent the right-center alliances from winning an absolute majority. The number of Communist deputies increased by 50 per cent (from 100 to 150) not because of votes for the extreme left (the percentage voting Communist remained about the same) but because of votes for the extreme right (if there had been fewer Poujadists in the country, there would have been fewer Communists in the Palais-Bourbon). By this dialectic, paradoxical at first sight and yet logical, the voters brought about results counter to their intentions. By voting for the Communists, who had been shut out of the political community since 1948, millions of Frenchmen gave the right the chance to rule. By voting for the Poujadists, other millions of Frenchmen, returning the courtesy of the Communists, ensured the investiture of Guy Mollet and the return of the Socialists to power.

The 1956 Assembly included about two hundred deputies stubbornly opposed to the system, and unconcerned about the smooth operation of constitutional institutions. There remained less than four hundred deputies to support a government—a hundred or so Socialists on one wing, and about a hundred Independents on the other, and between the two, the M.R.P. and a scattering of splinter parties short on both members and cohesion. If we recall that 10 to 15 per cent of the members of a majority are apt to change sides on important measures because of lack of party discipline, we must conclude that in the Assembly elected in 1956 only a coalition would be able to form and support a government, and that this coalition would have to include both the Socialists and the Independents: that is, the extreme left and the extreme right of the democratic parties.

It would be easy to blame both groups. Socialists and followers of Mendès-France, united in a would-be Republican Front, could not constitute a government majority alone. In their campaign they spread the false impression that there was an irresolvable conflict between the previous coalition and that of the morrow. After the election, they had to win the votes of those whom they had denounced the day before. The Republican Front set the stage for a ministerial crisis by alienating in advance an element of the inevitable majority. One might also blame the Poujadists, or rather their constituents, who, denouncing "the auctioneers of the Empire" and calling for war against the tax authorities, gave expression, grandiose and caricatural, to a national inconsistency. It is tempting to desire greatness and to balk at its price.

However one may censure the conduct of the leaders of the Republican Front and the Poujadist voters, the essential thing is the make-up of the Assembly, itself a reflection of the structure of the "system," a structure which in turn was inseparable from the attitude of the French citizen in matters of politics. Under the Fourth Republic, more than a third of the deputies in the three Assemblies of 1946, 1951, and 1956 did not play the game and were hostile to the constitutional system as it then stood. This third of extremists represented a group of voters which was regularly above 40 per cent, even above 45 per cent in 1951. The Fourth Republic never succeeded in winning over the people as a whole: at each election they voted for or against the "system" along with a policy within the framework of the established Constitution.

*   *   *

The way in which French parliamentary procedure operates has always been an object of astonishment for observers, and for specialists, deputies, and journalists a source of "poisons and delights."

The seemingly distinctive feature of French parliamentary government was, according to almost unanimous opinion, ministerial instability, more or less combined with the weakness of the executive power, and government by the legislature. Ministerial instability does not date from the Fourth Republic; it was already known and deplored under the Third, when the Chamber of Deputies included only a few members who were hostile to the regime. Consequently a distinction is called for: the French legislature, even when made up exclusively of "constitutional" deputies, did not avoid ministerial crises; and the latter, despite their frequency, did not endanger the survival of the constitutional system.

What is the reason for this ministerial instability which none of the French Republics has been able to curb? Perhaps the answer will be easier if we first try to find out how this instability has been prevented in different times and places.

In modern democracies all groups organize freely to express their opinions and defend their interests. The deputies are elected by all the citizens; the government, finally, must win the support of legislators sensitive to the complaints of their constituents and the claims of producers, consumers, and taxpayers. In such circumstances, administrations are compelled to listen to the dissonant, more or less passionate voices of these idio-collective interests. But the very existence of the government is not thereby endangered. The President of the United States is elected for four years, and nothing except death, illness, or voluntary resignation can put an end to his term of office. The British Prime Minister, since the number of parties has been reduced to two, has the constant support of a parliamentary majority subject to a strict discipline. Except in the case of a revolt within his party or of public opinion (the Suez crisis was the last example), the Prime Minister alone chooses the time for the dissolution of Parliament and new elections.

In the absence of a two-party system and of a presidential government, stability may be assured either when one of the several parties holds an absolute majority, either alone (as in Sweden), or with the assistance of a secondary party (the Socialist-Liberal coalition in Belgium), or when several parties form an alliance on a specific program for one term of a legislature (Holland). When none of these conditions is met, when the government depends on temporary and revocable agreements between numerous parties, no one of which is subject to discipline when it comes to the vote, a certain ministerial instability is unavoidable. During the last century, in the Chambre des Communes, governments came into being and died as a result of parliamentary battles—not without a certain amount of confusion. For instability to become understandable, it is enough to recall that the Palais-Bourbon never knew any organized, disciplined parties capable of making long-term agreements.

If there had been no parties at all the parliamentary game would have been dominated by the rivalry of a few leaders around whom groups of followers formed. If all parties had been of the same sort, with or without disciplined voting, a definite type of coalition would have emerged. But the French Assembly has always been composed not only of numerous parties but of heterogeneous parties as well. The executive committee of the Radical Party did not commit the Radical deputies, but in order to win the support of the Socialist deputies it was necessary to convince the *comité directeur,* itself sensitive to the wishes of the party militants. Parties were based, some on a more or less imaginary class concept (the Socialist Party), others on a religious ideal (the Popular Republican Party), some on temperament or on historical memories (the Radical Party), still others on an ill-defined conservatism (the Independents). How can we be surprised that none of them was united when it came to settling a real issue or choosing a head of government?

The structure of the French Assemblies has been the constant, necessary if not sufficient, cause of ministerial instability. It has given the functioning of the government its peculiar characteristic: an all-but-permanent state of strife. Everything took place as though the opposition were undertaking to upset the Cabinet a few days, a few weeks, or at most a few months after it had been formed. When the Assembly contained but a single majority, the government changed within the same majority. If there were several possible majorities, the orientation of the government would change without the voters having given the slightest indication of a change of mind. Democracy in France under the Third and Fourth Republics was a form of government in which the people delegated their sovereignty every four or five years to six hundred elected deputies, who disposed of it as they saw fit.

The legal concepts—rule by assembly, parliamentary government, separation of powers—are extremely equivocal. Only in the United States has Montesquieu's formula on the separation of powers, probably misinterpreted, been expressed in the institutions of government. In Great Britain, the executive and legislature have a common origin, the same composition. Practice, based on tradition and the structure of the parties, gives the Cabinet the capacity for decision and freedom of action. In France, despite legend, the Assembly was no more able to govern than elsewhere, and at times measures of considerable importance were not submitted to it (for example, it never debated the Monnet Plan). However, since a cohesive and lasting majority was lacking, the mandate given the government was always revocable. During these last two years the mandate had become so precarious that the members of the Assembly did not hesitate to intervene in diplomatic negotiations. Let us not forget, nevertheless, that this last stage of disintegration was to be blamed less on French parliamentary government and its rooted customs than on exceptional circumstances.

The permanent nature of the struggle for power bred uncertainty concerning both men and action. Who would be premier tomorrow? What would the next government do in Morocco, or in Algeria? To make a prediction, it was necessary to haunt the corridors of the Palais-Bourbon and chat with the different groups. The deputies participated in secret rites, played an esoteric game: they belonged to a sect both secret and open. They were representatives of the people, of course, but they were following also a unique trade, the parliamentary profession.

A quarter of a century ago André Tardieu studied and denounced the parliamentary profession. Two sociologists, one French and the other American, recently wrote a book on the ways of deputies and senators as observed at the time of an election to the Presidency of the Republic.[1]

All professional politicians, in all countries, develop special characteristics: there is a "personal equation" for a deputy in the same way that there is one for a doctor or professor. This equation is probably more marked in the case of a French deputy because the mores of the Palais-Bourbon tended to magnify the occupational traits into an absurd caricature. The deputy becomes different from other citizens not insofar as he is a legislator or administrator, but as a candidate for elective office, as interpreter of the grievances and claims of individuals and groups to the public authorities, and finally, as a contestant in the struggle for honors and positions.

Deputies have a tendency to confuse an election speech with the statement of a problem or solution. Journalists and civil servants are duty bound, in a government dictated by opinion, to limit the influence of this inevitable distortion. The politician nevertheless has an indispensable function to perform as an intermediary between the governed and the governors, explaining to the former the purposes and motives of the latter, and making known at the top the hopes and aspirations of "the base." The danger of perversion is implicit in the function. The deputy or minister who conceived

[1] C. Melnik and N. Leites, *The House Without Windows* (New York, 1958).

of his role according to Alain's teaching would consider himself solely a messenger of the simple citizens and would forget his responsibility in the expression of a general will, in the protection of the common good.

Were French parliamentarians less concerned about the national interest than deputies were in other countries? It is hard to express a categorical opinion on a subject which by its very nature evades close examination. The almost unanimous opinion that the French deputy was more of a slave than his colleague in other countries is explained by the structure of the legislature and parties. In democratic politics individuals do not know complete independence (except for a few outstanding personalities or unambitious lookers-on). The less the deputy is bound by party discipline the less he resists pressure groups. Contrary to what so many lovers of individualism believe, isolation delivers the elected representative to all sorts of temptation. Of course, organized parties are sensitive to the wishes of the classes which provide their electoral support. At least they are not all sensitive to the wishes of the same classes and are capable of resistance, thanks to their collective strength. The lone deputy, who seems to depend on no one, ends all too often by depending (or imagining that he depends) on everyone.

Nevertheless, the special psychology of the French deputy seems to me to have been not so much the cause as the result of the system. Among Western legislators, only the French deputy took part in an execution (the overthrowing of a Cabinet), in a festivity (ministerial crisis), and in a prize-giving ceremony (the formation of a Cabinet), every three, six, or twelve months. In the interval between these ceremonies he was recovering from the last one, and getting ready for the next.

Not that the "ceremony"—ministerial crisis or election of the President of the Republic—is peculiar to French parliamentary government. The study we alluded to above, devoted to the election of René Coty, gives one the feeling less of something unique than of the perfecting of a genre or the stylizing of practices which are in themselves normal. A parallel automatically suggests itself: the choice by the American parties of candidates for President of the United States.

The similarities are many and immediately discernible. In both instances, elected delegates or deputies have to choose by election one man from among several candidates. Some candidates have made public announcements, others are in reserve, biding their time. Among the delegates, some obey strictly the directives of the group to which they belong, while others retain their freedom of choice. The groups are heterogeneous, some large and compact, others small, and always on the verge of break-up. In cases where the principal groups are evenly balanced and no candidate can obtain an absolute majority, small groups can tip the scales one way or the other and play a part out of proportion to their proper weight. A dark horse may triumph, expressing less the real preference than the resignation of the majority.

Aside from the language and style of the participants, the development of the presidential election of 1953 with its successive stages, carefully differentiated by the "Bourbonologues," hardly offers anything strikingly original. The groups are too numerous to agree in advance, they are not united enough to foresee the outcome of a trial of strength, they are forced to "lift the mortgages," that is, to show that a certain individual cannot win the necessary number of votes.[2] These polls take time and slowly change the atmosphere until general impatience and the weariness of those whose hopes have been deceived force a solution.

Some of the expressions we have just used apply to the search for a premier as well as for a President of the Republic and remind us of those disconcerting rites which, depending on time and country, stirred up irritation, irony, or indignation: "once around the track" (one individual who knows he has no chance spends several days

---

[2] And thus eliminate (lift) the claim (mortgages) held by a pretender to the premiership on the new government. The idiom "lever les hypothèques" is indicative of the role played by property in France. (L.E.)

in conversations devoid of significance), "lift the mortgages" (an individual whose chances are few but not inexistent tries an experiment so that the number of possible solutions will be gradually narrowed down to the conclusion). These rites had originally a reasonably intelligible function: the lack of discipline in the groups did not allow the leaders to come to an understanding because none of them knew the exact number of votes he could count on. Gradually the function was forgotten and the ceremonial aspect became dominant. And yet, the ceremony retained a psychological function: since the new Cabinet would inevitably resemble the former one, men had to forget previous quarrels so as to prepare for the morrow's understanding.

It is easy to see that both French public opinion and foreign observers would gradually become exasperated by the repetition of crises each of which required several weeks of settling. But it would be too easy to blame the "politician's deformity" alone. The major fact is that the deputies, because of the structure of the system, were waging a perennial battle for power. This battle, which under the present British form of government is fought in all its violence only at the time of general elections, which under the American system comes once every four years, in the election of the President, and in an attenuated form every two years in the congressional elections; this battle was renewed under the French system every time there was a ministerial crisis.

There were times under the Third Republic (1928–1932), or even under the Fourth Republic (1948–1951), when governments might have lasted, since a single parliamentary majority was possible. André Tardieu did not forgive the professional politicians for frustrating his efforts without, to him, any valid reason except the deformity which comes as a result of a parliamentary career. After the expulsion of the Communists from the government in 1947, the majority was made up necessarily of Socialists and Popular Republicans, plus a fraction, more or less large, of others, Radicals and moderates.

But since 1932 France has usually been faced with issues whose gravity would have tested any regime: how was the economic depression to be alleviated? What policy was to be adopted toward the Third Reich? After the Liberation the questions were neither less numerous nor less pressing: what was to be the attitude toward the Communist Party? toward European unity? How was France to preserve, transform, or abandon the French Union? In twenty-five years neither the country at large nor the politicians ever gave a unanimous answer to these fateful questions. France, herself, was as deeply divided as her governing classes. Our form of government, because of its structure, tended to enlarge real disagreements, multiplying them by the quarrels among the professional politicians.

For twenty-five years every party, except the Communist Party, which is Russian-controlled, has split each time a vital issue has come up. Every party has had, in variable proportions, members for and against the Munich agreement, Vichyists and Gaullists, members for and against a United Europe, and partisans of negotiation and of pacification in Algeria. Consequently, disagreement on immediate problems was added to the traditional dissensions. Public opinion continued to rail against parties which had ceased to exist as units.

In such circumstances the parliamentary game developed a complexity which discouraged all but the expert. There was no longer any need to change the majority in order to change the policy. The representatives of two opposing policies—Pierre Laval and Paul Reynaud—might have occupied the same Moderate bench, had they belonged to the same Assembly. Georges Mandel and Georges Bonnet were members of the same Cabinet. Robert Schuman and Georges Bidault were members of the same party, but the replacement of Schuman by Bidault represented a subtle shift in diplomacy (Bidault was less "European" than Schuman). At this time all the consequences of the coexistence of half-disciplined and totally undisciplined parties appeared. In order to form a Cabinet the consent of the central committees of certain parties and also the votes of enough deputies voting independently were necessary. The choice of each cabinet member took on significance. Not only did the representatives of each of the traditional groups have to be in balance (right, left, Socialist, Radical, moderate), but also those of the non-official groups ("Europeans" and "non-Europeans," "Ultras" and liberals). The difficulty of getting a majority in order to form a Cabinet or to approve a decision became such that the concern over parliamentary consent finally obscured the basic issues. The deputies were as though shut up in a house without doors or windows, inextricably involved in their own schemings. This impression was misleading. During periods of calm, the professionals were responsible for crises—for a whole generation they had been giving expression to them; perhaps they aggravated them; all too often they could not resolve them; but they did not create them.

Haunted by the need for a majority, the Premier, as we have said, was inclined to confuse the solution of the parliamentary problem (how to maintain a majority?) with the solution of the real issue (what to do in Algeria?). Insofar as the politicians were unable to adopt a solution or even to accept any policy at all, the Premier was tempted to heed a diabolical piece of advice: to create or permit certain *faits accomplis* to which the deputies would be obliged to yield. Consciously or not, this technique was used during the Moroccan emergency in 1955. M. Grandval hoped to take the initiative and impose a solution, compromising beween the maintenance of Sultan Ben Arafa on the throne and the return of Sultan Ben Youssef. The "Ultras" fought Grandval to a standstill and lost the opportunity (perhaps a poor one) for reforms which would not have entailed the immediate end of the protectorate. By repeated concessions to the "Ultras," by delay, the Cabinet, intentionally or not, gave way to events which forced it to go further than even its most liberal members had at first contemplated. Who was responsible for the outcome? The "Ultras," who had prevented a last tentative conciliation within the structure of the protectorate, or the liberals, who had started the inevitably revolutionary movement? The matter is open to debate.

*   *   *

This discussion brings us automatically to further questions: why so many weak and heterogeneous parties? Why so many extremists of both right and left?

Let us begin with a common-sense statement: a plurality of parties, not the two-party system, is natural. If nothing obliges them, or at least incites them, voters and their representatives will not organize themselves into two blocs, but will instead scatter into many different parties. Now, the two chief factors in this organization are the electoral law and the functioning of the legislature. Since 1789, and even since 1871, we have tested many electoral systems, but never the only two which could have eliminated splinter parties or brought about a synthesis: the English method of election by simple majority in single-member constituencies whose direct simplicity pitilessly eliminates "marginal" individuals or groups, and proportional representation with the clause adopted by the German Federal Republic, by which parties not winning 5 per cent of the votes throughout the whole country have no right to a seat. Proportional representation biased in favor of the big parties one time, another time favoring the little ones, election by double ballot in single-member constituencies, election by double ballot of lists on a *département* basis—none of these laws (not even the last one, which applied only once) obliged the candidates to follow the party policies, or the voters to confine their votes to the candidate of one party. The mixed system, in which some candidates owed their election to their personal position in the district or *département,* others to the success of a party, was never overcome. This mixed system at the electoral level corresponds exactly to the mixed system at the parliamentary level. In electoral districts as at the Palais-Bourbon, the political struggle was sometimes one of individuals, sometimes one of parties. In both cases it appeared as a conflict of ideas, and usually it brought to grips both parties and men—parties divided in everything but traditional preferences and men whose quarrels did not always express the clash of ideas. The quarrel of the two Edouards (Edouard Herriot and Edouard Daladier), both members of the Radical Party, was in no way a matter of philosophical principle. The realignment of "personalities" during these last few years offers innumerable occasions for astonishment. Bidault and Soustelle, opposed yesterday as chiefs of the M.R.P. (Popular Republican Movement) and R.P.F., one for and the other against the E.D.C., found themselves in complete agreement when it came to the defense of "French Algeria."

In the House of Commons, the concept of government and opposition contributed to the formation of two mass parties. In the United States the method of voting, the exigencies of the presidential election, the organization of committees and of the processes of legislation as a party function, along majority and minority lines, have prevented the innumerable movements and sects from ever rising to national prominence. The equivalent of the French profusion of parties has appeared, but only inside each party and in the different states.

Neither the electoral laws nor parliamentary rules have set up any barrier to the proliferation of parties in France; they have merely reflected it. The statement is debatable: the electoral and legislative practices may be considered the cause and the multiplicity of parties the effect. It is a question of two complementary aspects of the same phenomenon. Jean Jacques Rousseau wrote that "it is precisely because the force of events always tends to destroy equality, that the force of law must always tend to maintain it." One might say similarly that the greater the tendency in a free society for factions to multiply, the more legislation must favor the organization of but a few strong parties.

Admitting this weakness on the part of the legislators, are the French more heterogeneous, more susceptible to division, than other European countries? All the Catholic or predominantly Catholic countries—France, Spain, Italy, the Latin American countries—find it hard to adapt parliamentary institutions of British origin. There seems to be some sort of relation between religious pluralism and the two-party system in politics, and between the more or less exclusive domination of one church and political pluralism. This relationship could not be considered a scientific law, but the reasons for it and its origin are vaguely apparent. The opposition between right and left in France coincides to a certain extent with that between the adherents of the Church and the laity (not to say believers and rationalists). The importance of the religious question (for or against clericalism, the Church, parochial schools) prevents, on the right, the organization of a large moderate party which would include Voltairists and Catholics, and on the left it creates a solidarity, traditional but today illusory, among liberals, Socialists and Communists. Moreover, those who stand opposed to a Universal Church with a dogmatic theology accept the Communist counter-religion more readily than do Anglo-Saxon nonconformists. The French party system is different from both that in Italy and the system which existed in Republican Spain. A few common traits may be nonetheless found: a left divided into at least three branches, Communists, Socialists, and rationalists (liberal or radical), and a right which, in not being unified into a single party of Catholic inspiration (a feat accomplished in Italy after the Second World War), is also composed of three sections: the anticlerical conservatives, those imbued with the Catholic or Christian spirit, and those opposed to the democratic or republican order. These six groups make up what may be called the spontaneous expression of political attitudes in a predominantly Catholic country, with the left-wing rationalists and the anticlerical conservatives likely either to merge, or, on the contrary, to form more than two splinter parties.

The dialectic style of the party system in a Catholic country has developed in France with a few national peculiarities neither more nor less mysterious than those of other nations. The Communist Party gained considerable electoral power as a result of its role in the Resistance and Liberation. The center and constitutional right groups have never achieved a solid organization, either in the Assembly or in the country at large. For a half-century the fluctuations of our history have all been conducive to division rather than to consolidation.

In 1945-46, just after the Liberation, a combination of circumstances, General de Gaulle's prestige, proportional representation, and fear of Communism, led to the appearance of the Popular Republican Movement, the large moderate party the experts had long hoped for. First the R.P.F., and then traditional conservatism drew their strength from the circumstantially inflated forces of the Popular Republicans. The latter after a few years were back to their traditional constituencies in a few well-defined regions (Brittany, the Département du Nord, Alsace, and a few *départements* in the west). Supporters of the M.R.P., some conservative, others more liberal, are almost all recruited in the provinces where Catholic sentiment is still deeply rooted.

The development of a Christian Democratic party incapable of taking the place occupied by its sister parties in Germany and Italy could only add to the pluralism and the confusion. A deplorable phenomenon certainly, but one hard to avert, since nothing, either in the electoral law or in the parliamentary regulations, tended to prevent this proliferation. In all countries organized parties have arisen on the left rather than on the right. The right has answered a threat, responded to a challenge. As long as it is not forced, the right prefers an individualistic to a collective party structure. Even today it is good form to plead for the single-member constituency in order to protect representatives from the "tyranny of the parties," and "bring them closer to the voters," as though the so-called independence of six hundred deputies would lead to an efficient parliament. Counter to the whole development of modern societies, the moderates still yearn in large numbers for an Assembly of personalities.

This attitude is not explained merely by an attachment to a more or less legendary past. Economically and socially, France is more heterogeneous than Great Britain, though less so than Italy. The difference between the regions north and south of the Loire is less marked than that between the Po basin and the provinces of the defunct kingdom of Naples. Nevertheless, French industry is still concentrated in a few areas (Paris and its gradually spreading environs, the north and east around the two coal basins, the regions of Lyon-Saint-Etienne, Marseilles, and Grenoble). Aside from these complexes we hardly find anything but secondary centers (Norman iron-smelting, shipbuilding at Nantes, Saint-Nazaire, and around Bordeaux and Toulouse) and light industries scattered among mainly agricultural provinces. Whole regions in the west, southwest, and southeast have kept the old ways of life. Why should politics have changed its style and be subject to the dictates of the masses and of organizations? The socio-economic diversity of the country, which has not prevented the development of movements on a national scale, has had two main consequences: it has been reflected among supporters of each of the great parties (the Communists recruit votes among the farmers and tenant farmers in poor agricultural *départements* as well as among workers in *départements* in full industrial expansion), and it has crystallized the multiple expressions of center and right, assuring the solidity of a party such as the M.R.P., which became regional.

Again, the foregoing account is a description rather than a causal analysis. But probably the very notion of cause has little bearing on such a subject. A cause might be said to be the factor which, if present, would have made inevitable, and if absent, would have rendered impossible, the phenomenon we wish to explain. Neither the electoral statutes, the multiplicity of ideologies, or the socio-economic diversity raised any insurmountable barrier to a system of a few well-organized parties. No one could maintain that it would be enough to eliminate one of these factors (and how eliminate the multiplicity of ideologies?) for the political scene to be simplified and for the functioning of the regime to become more efficient. The fact remains that the nature of these elements is in harmony with the multiparty system. That system is the product of a Catholic country whose varied regions have evolved differently, whose individuals cling to contradictory politico-metaphysical convictions—a country where the vote is dominated by traditions or by ideas as much as it is by clearly recognized interests, either private or collective. Whatever one may say, if democracy requires the representatives to express the wishes of the electors, then the composition of the Assemblies was in singular conformity with the ideal.

And yet in France more than in any country in Europe people speak of the disparity between "legal" France and the real country. During the last years of the Fourth Republic people were always denouncing the "alienation" of the professional politicians, lost amid oversubtle schemings which the ordinary citizen failed to grasp and which he watched with growing irritation. That the crisis, which had become an almost permanent condition in 1957–58, was severely criticized by Frenchmen is certain. Most certainly, it was not what they wanted. This does not mean that the Assembly, as constituted, reflected a distorted image of the nation.

Either knowingly or through a misunderstanding, the voters sent to the Palais-Bourbon more than 150 Communist deputies and about 50 Poujadists. More than five million Frenchmen voted for the Communist Party, more than two million for candidates representing Pierre Poujade, whose mode of speech would make Hitler's sound cultivated by comparison. In January 1956, the French got the Assembly they earned on election day.

Can it be said that these deputies betrayed the wishes or opinions of those who had elected them? Alas, no! On the whole, public-opinion polls show the same attitudes on main issues among the public as among the deputies. The Poujadist voter is against taxation and for a greater France with the same ingenuousness or cynicism as displayed in the *Aurore* (although he is normally more naive and less cynical than Robert Bony). As for those voting Communist, most of them would probably abhor the regimes of Stalin or Khrushchev, but if we go by their answers to the poll-takers, two thirds of them think, or at least talk, as the Communist leaders desire. The politicians may be responsible for the fact that moderates and liberals vote for a half-dozen different parties or groups. But the political elite alone cannot be blamed for the fact that the party openly obeying orders from Moscow and the candidates offered by a rabble-rouser together obtained 40 per cent of the votes.

Is the tendency to vote for the extremes a typically French trait? It has often been said that it is a question of verbal and ideological extremism easily reconciled with an underlying conservatism. Because of the structure of the parliamentary game, the vote does not indicate the voter's choice of a government or policy, but rather the expression of a state of mind. Dissatisfied on principle, the Frenchman tends to vote *against*. The parties of the extremes satisfy this need for opposition.

This interpretation is not without truth, but it does allow for another explanation of a historical nature. All the regimes of the last century were weak because none of them gained the support of the political class as a whole, nor was any one of them founded on the firmly loyal support of the French people.

During the last century France hestitated among three regimes: a monarchy more or less adapted to the ideals of the Revolution, a republic, and, last, a substitute for monarchy, the prince-president or emperor appealing to the principle of democratic legitimacy, retaining an elected Assembly and universal suffrage but arrogating to himself a more or less absolute power of decision. From 1815 on, the French never gave evidence of either sharp opposition or unreserved loyalty to any of these three or four regimes. The two monarchies were overthrown by Parisian riots, transformed into revolutions by the sovereigns' weakness and the desertion of a fraction of the political class. The Empire, even in its declining days, had been ratified by universal suffrage, and was overthrown only by military disaster. The Republic became firmly established in one generation, but it had been endangered by a general who based his claim on future victories.

Between the end of the nineteenth century and 1930, conservative opposition to the Republic had almost disappeared, and opposition from the Communist left was not yet a serious threat. For the past twenty-five years, however, the regime has once again been constantly challenged. That it failed to resist the catastrophe of 1940 is not astonishing: in our century governments do not withstand defeat or even the mere consciousness of defeat. The Fourth Republic was a restoration after an interlude of authoritarian rightist revolutions.

The Fourth Republic was attacked from the right first by the Rally of the French People (R.P.F.) with a program similar to that of Boulangism, centered on the theme of constitutional reform, and then by Poujadism. The two movements are much less alike than has been claimed. The partisans of the latter—as sociological studies of the election have shown—are not the same as the supporters of the R.P.F. (as near as can be ascertained, less than half the Poujade supporters voted for the R.P.F. in 1951). The style of General de Gaulle resembles that of the stationer of Saint-Céré as much as the château of Versailles resembles the corner grocery. But the diversity of the two rightist opposition parties confirms one facet of the national psychology: the readiness of a part of the country to give its electoral support and sometimes even its heart to a man or movement defined politically by hostility to the parliamentary system. A democratic regime is stabilized when individuals, groups, and parties try to settle their grievances and realize their aspirations without redebating the form of government itself. In France, for nearly two centuries, every national emergency has automatically caused a constitutional crisis.

There was little to be feared from Poujadism itself. Its leader's mediocrity, the emptiness of its program, the ineffectiveness of the policy it adopted, kept it from increasing the number of its supporters, as the Fascist or National-Socialist parties had done a generation earlier. Warm feeling, noble ideals, both altogether necessary to a rightist revolution in industrial societies where materialism rules during time of peace, were lacking in this almost burlesque movement whose leaders resembled the mass and which, united from top to bottom more in hatred of taxation than in love of greatness, resolved to "kick the rascals out" or to get rid of the *polyvalents*[3] rather than to sacrifice themselves for the recovery of the empire.

---

[3] A treasury agent particularly entrusted with collecting taxes from groups and people reluctant to pay them. (L.E.)

Poujadism had both meaning and consequences nonetheless. It provoked the moderate right to demagogy and exaggeration. By preventing the working of the political alliances (*apparentements*) it increased the parliamentary strength of the Communists and was partly responsible for the composition of an ungovernable Assembly. Finally—and this is perhaps the main thing—it brought into the open an often-misunderstood social mechanism: economic progress creates as many demands as it satisfies.

Let us recall the situation at the beginning of 1956. France had just experienced three years of exceptional prosperity, of increasing stability in prices, with her foreign exchange in balance. Real wages had increased from 15 to 20 per cent in three years—an abnormally rapid increase. Yet in the 1956 elections nearly 40 per cent of the vote was against the system. Expansion had not appeased wage earners but had irritated thousands of independent workers, businessmen, craftsmen, tenant farmers, and land-owning peasants.

There is always the danger that economic growth will involve hardship, especially in a country where the working population is not increasing. In these circumstances it operates by transfer—of labor toward more productive activities, and of population to areas where development is favored by geographic or economic factors. Stagnant regions as a result undergo a relative, at times absolute, decline. Those remaining in the less favored zones are embittered, especially those engaged in tertiary services, particularly merchants, who are doomed by the slackening of activity. It was south of the Loire, toward the middle of the country and the southwest that the stationer of Saint-Céré made the first moves to which he owed his fame and where his movement had its greatest successes.

But the movement spread to the rest of the country and won, in certain *départements* undertaking rapid industrial expansion, a percentage of votes equal to or above its national average. Studies suggest an explanation of the same sort, but different in detail: some groups feel that they are victims of fate and of the State in a period of prosperity. The number of such victims, or those who so consider themselves, is especially great because France contains many "marginals," independent persons who struggle to maintain a traditional way of work and life. It is also likely that the protests against excessive taxation were often more justified than was believed in the cities. French taxes are heavy when strictly paid. They are insupportable when they strike areas or professions on the decline. Even if they are equitable in the abstract and represent a normal share of over-all national expenditures, they are resented as unjust if they force reconversion of out-of-date enterprises in accordance with the wishes of economists but contrary to the desires—and they too are legitimate—of the interested parties. Elsewhere these protests would have been expressed through party or professional organizations. In France the double tradition of peasant resistance to taxation and of hostility to the regime favored the Poujadist expression of discontent.

The vote of more than five million Frenchmen for the Communists poses a similar problem in collective psychology. The explanation citing low wages or standard of living is oddly superficial, if not false: real wages of laborers are higher than those of Dutch workers, and at least equal to those in Germany. It is true that some suffer from bad housing. But the well-housed in the north and east still continue to cast their votes for Communist candidates. Psycho-sociological studies of Communist support are far from agreement in their final conclusions. We shall try to sort out what seems to be both certain and essential.

Analysis of election returns combined with polls of public opinion make it possible to describe in detail the social make-up of Communist support. About half of it comes from industrial workers, and the other half is recruited from all social strata—peasants, merchants, craftsmen, civil servants, and so on. Geographically the party's strongholds are in the industrial zones (around Paris and the Département du Nord), but also in predominantly agricultural areas which may be likened to underdeveloped areas (the Creuse district, for instance), and, finally, in localities of the southeast, where it apparently owes its success as much to leftist tradition as to proletarian spirit, or a revolt against stagnation. The diversity of the sociological sources of strength and of their geographical distribution does not exclude deviations among various constituencies or social classes. But nowhere does the strength fall below 10 per cent, nor does it anywhere noticeably exceed a third of the votes. The most characteristic feature of this electorate is neither professional nor geographic: by far the great majority of Communist voters are recruited among those having low or mediocre incomes. Tocqueville saw in the French Revolution a vast protest against social inequality, the inequality expressed in the estates. Perhaps he would see Communism today as a vast protest against economic inequality.

Why does this protest assume, in France, but not in Great Britain or Germany, the form of allegiance to Communism, at least in electoral terms? One of the answers most often given by Frenchmen wishing to reassure their friends from across the Channel or the Atlantic is that these five million voters are not really Communists, but that they are like the left-wing Labourites in England (Mr. Bevan's faithful) and that they mistake the nature and aims of the Communist Party. This interpretation seems to me, on the basis of existing studies, both true and false.

If they mean that these five million Frenchmen are more like their compatriots than they are like the militant Stalinists who control the party Central Committee, they are right. A vote for the Communist candidate implies neither belief in the dogma nor unconditional obedience to the orders of a party which acts under orders from Moscow. Probably most of these Frenchmen would abhor government by a "people's democracy." Possibly some of them are somewhat fearful and do not want their ballots to bring to power those for whom they have voted. It has been shown that workers who are on the rolls of the C.G.T. (*Confédération Général du Travail*) and who vote the Communist slates are not ready to lose a few days' pay to demonstrate against the coup d'état in Algiers or General de Gaulle's coming to power.

This having been said, it would, as I see it, be a mistake to conclude that Communist voters are Socialists who do not know themselves. If this were true, French workers would be appreciably more unintelligent or less informed than their brothers across the Channel or the Rhine. Nothing allows passing such judgment on the "most intelligent people on earth." In certain respects a large proportion of Communist voters—two thirds, according to the polls—are indeed convinced Communists.

They imagine history as the Soviets try to describe it. Between 10 and 20 per cent of Frenchmen believe that the danger of war comes from the United States rather than from the Soviet Union, that the former is more imperialist than the latter. In case of conflict they would hope for victory by the East rather than the West. One may question the sincerity of these answers if one wishes: even—and above all, if—they are not sincere, they confirm the success of the Communist effort which in effect aims at indoctrinating individuals and masses, at setting up verbal reflexes as well as spreading ideas.

These millions of Frenchmen are still Communists, although in a less strict sense; to the extent that, though unsatisfied with the party, they are not resigned to abandoning it and transferring their votes to another leftist candidate. What are the motives for this fidelity? The feeling that capitalism, as such, is bad and that only communism opposes it? The consciousness of belonging to an exploited class whose only spokesman is the Communist Party, in spite of Khrushchev's talk and the events at Budapest? An attitude, rooted in a long history, of hostility to the State and a refusal to fit into the framework of present society? The need for a revolutionary ideal, a refusal to be content with the prosaic quality of trade union or political reformism? The habit of voting *against,* which a population of grumblers has not lost and does not wish to lose?

The Russian Communist Party has domesticated the parties depending on it everywhere in the world, but nowhere has this servility been carried as far as in France. Stalinized, the Communist parties in the West, especially in France, are a social phenomenon almost without precedent. In theory and verbally they are revolutionary. In their structure and organization they are bureaucratic and bourgeois, as are inevitably all revolutionary movements a generation after their victories. The domination of the Russian party over world Communism has communicated certain features and distortions resulting from the exercise of power to all parties, even those still in opposition. The French Communist Party, frozen in its inexpiable and momentarily sterile hatred of the State and of formal society, changes young people in revolt against whatever *is* into mere filing clerks or pen-pushers. It would have become a factor for stability for the Fourth Republic if an electoral statute had cut down its parliamentary representation.

Observers have always been struck by the curious mixture, in the political behavior of the French, of conservatism and extremism. Individuals and groups obstinately defend their interests or traditions. All regimes, the Bourbon and Orléans monarchies, the Third and then the Fourth Republics, have seemed equally incapable of putting into practice the reforms which would have saved them. The resistance of the privileged classes—nobles or deputies—has always brought out the weakness of the state and finally made way for sudden collapse. Revolutionary protest vainly accompanies a paralysis which is ultimately more responsible for revolutions than are theorists or ideologies.

*   *   *

Discussion of the consequences of ministerial instability has been no less lively than discussion of its origins. Was it the origin of the ills of French politics? Was all hope of improvement vain as long as governments had no guaranteed life span? Was the instability the cause or the symptom; was it superficial or rooted?

The customs of the French Parliament obviously were not lacking in disadvantages. Lacking a certain future, ministers were unable to conceive and apply a long-term program, and inclined to leave their successors the worry of proceeding along unpopular lines or of settling difficult issues. The Premier became lost, so to speak, in anonymity: instead of being directly or indirectly chosen by universal suffrage and the head of a great party as in Great Britain or the United States, in France he was only one deputy among many, chosen by the President of the Republic or by the Assembly itself to reconcile temporarily the contradictory claims of groups and individuals. Finally, the frequency of crises ended by destroying the prestige of the regime in the eyes of the French, and the prestige of France in the world. The list of complaints was long.

But the replies, equally classic, to this indictment do not lack weight. During normal times the French form of government carried with it the double stability of solid administration and of ministerial personnel. The ministers changed less often than the premiers, and the administrators less often than the ministers. Is the conclusion to be that France was "administered and not governed"? Indeed, economic and social policy in France was, as in all democracies, the product of arbitration among interests, at times of compromise between national needs and public opinion. As for the conduct of foreign affairs, it seemed by turns, without change of regime, set aside for one man (or one party), then abandoned to an unfettered rivalry. Aristide Briand remained minister for seven years. From 1946 to 1953, the M.R.P., with Robert Schuman and Georges Bidault, occupied the Quai d'Orsay almost uninterruptedly.

As we look back over the last thirty years we see that the most serious errors were the doing of the governing class, of public opinion, and of the country itself. Heroically, absurdly, all the governments from 1931 to 1936 refused to devalue the currency, a measure absolutely necessary for economic recovery. In domestic affairs, at least, the nation was almost united in plunging headlong, first into deflation (1931–1936), then inflation (1936–1938).

On the other hand, France was irreconcilably divided on important questions which, in foreign affairs, involved her destiny. From 1933 to 1939 every international crisis—Ethiopia, the reoccupation of the Rhineland, Czechoslovakia—set off a great debate. But it was the same in England, whose diplomatic policy during that period was neither more farsighted nor more resolute than that of France.

Inquiry as to the consequences of governmental instability under the Fourth Republic leads to a series of questions which have no answers: would stronger governments have averted the war in Indochina? would they have entered sooner into negotiations with the Viet Minh? The provisional government of General de Gaulle had sent an expeditionary force, and although General Leclerc was in favor of an accord with Ho Chi Minh, another Gaullist, Admiral Thierry d'Argenlieu, bears a great responsibility for the onset of the war. In retrospect, we reproach the succession of governments from 1947 to 1954 with the steadiness of purpose worthy of a better fate in so far, at least, as Indochina is concerned. Are we to conclude that this steadfastness was the result of a lack of authority and tenure on the part of those at the helm? Doubt persists.

As for French public opinion, by 1958 it was no longer in doubt. It was to the system—that is, the Parliament and the members of Parliament—that responsibility for the national failure and, above all, the loss of empire, was attributed. Whereas world opinion was convinced that France's mistake had been to wage war in Indochina, or, at least, to persist in it after the Communist victory in China, the French themselves, victims of propaganda and their collective vanity, blamed their disappointments in Asia and Africa on those who had been in power since 1945. The fall of the Fourth Republic and the advent of de Gaulle to power led, in November and December of 1958, to the election of an Assembly as coherent as the one in 1956 was ungovernable. But the nation had changed less than its government, and in the very act of re-electing its legislature gave evidence of its enduring character.

If proportional representation had been applied, the Chamber of 1958 would have been like the one in 1951, if not that of 1956. In spite of the losses they suffered, the Communists would probably have remained the largest party, with about 19 per cent of the votes. There would have been a conservative majority, as was the case from

1951 to 1956, but it would have had to include the Independents, the Union for the New Republic (U.N.R.), and the M.R.P., if not small center groups. The shift in votes (the decrease of the Communist percentage from 25 to 19, the strength gained by the Independents, the sudden swelling of the U.N.R. votes, smaller on the first ballot than those of the R.P.F. in 1951), did not exceed similar fluctuation experienced in stabilized democracies. French voters are neither more nor less changeable than voters in other countries. The change in the political arena has three causes: changes in constitutional regulations, a typical French phenomenon since 1789, the influence of electoral procedure on the composition of the Assemblies, and the sudden appearance of an improvised party, the U.N.R., which, appealing to the prestige of its great leader, succeeded in uniting in its favor the elements of public opinion against the outgoing members, and for General de Gaulle and a French Algeria. More than two hundred U.N.R. deputies with the collaboration of the members from Algeria, will easily dominate the legislature.

It has been proven that a divided country can, with favorable laws and conditions, and by rallying around a man of prestige, provide itself with an apparently united legislative body. Those profiting by the "Revolution of May" will perhaps stay in power for some years, just as the profiteers of the Liberation stayed in power for twelve. But if the "poisons and delights" of the system belong to the past, if the relapse into the parliamentary anarchy of yesterday is unlikely, the future of democracy in France remains still uncertain. Underneath the Gaullist quasi-unanimity, divisions still exist. By voting for the unknown the French have again voted against the world as it is. The Fifth Republic begins as a "parliamentary empire."

III ❊

MYTHS AND REALITIES
OF THE FRENCH ECONOMY

THE French economy has a bad reputation abroad. So peculiar does the economy appear that the best observers end by changing it entirely on pretext of describing it. According to M. Lüthy, France, it seems, has had "generations of technical and organizational stagnation." [1] Let us answer with a few figures: from 1901 to 1913, per-capita industrial production increased 57 per cent, a rate higher than the one for Europe (37 per cent), or even for Germany. From 1920 to 1929, per-capita industrial production grew by 31 per cent, that for Europe by 18 per cent. Finally, from 1938 to 1955, the increase in per-capita industrial production was 47 per cent, while the average for the countries of the O.E.E.C. (Organization for European Economic Cooperation) was 52 per cent. But the exceptionally rapid progress in 1956, 1957, and 1958 (an annual increase of about 10 per cent in industrial production) has, as of the present moment, raised the French figure above the average of the O.E.E.C.

There was a period, on the other hand, during which French industrial production did not keep up with the world-wide trend. During the ten years from 1930 to 1939, per-capita industrial production fell 14 per cent, while it increased about 25 per cent in neighboring countries. When the results of the last half-century are compared, one is tempted to make France an exception, but the

[1] Herbert Lüthy, *France Against Herself* (New York, 1955), p. 302.

reason is not a constant state of inertia, or regular but abnormally slow progress: it was the French inability to emerge from the depression of 1930, the prolongation of the slump for a decade which, combined with the years of war and occupation, caused a lag not yet overcome.

The French landscape and sometimes even statistics may convey an impression of stagnation. There are regions where industry has, so to speak, not penetrated, and which have kept the charm and anachronistic ways of the peasantry of tradition. Sleepy villages and small towns inspire both variations on the theme of *immobilisme* by observers who pride themselves on their economics, and touching remarks about eternal France by votaries of the good old preindustrial days. We may add that the lack of population increase cannot fail to be reflected in the figures. If gross figures on production or national product of different countries are compared without taking population changes into account, the country where the population is not increasing, as is the case in France, appears economically paralyzed.

Observers also tend to believe that common occurrences become extraordinary in the French context. Here again, M. Lüthy offers us a choice example. "The inflation," he wrote in 1952, "has long since ceased to be a technical financial question . . ." [2] As Lüthy saw it, it had become a social or psychological phenomenon, a kind of chronic disease of society. The National Commission of Accounting (*Commission des Comptes de la Nation*) had explained in its first report why the French economy, with a relatively rigid production structure, a large number of small business concerns, and "bottlenecks" in some key products (meat, for example), was particularly vulnerable to inflation. Governments are often inclined, through weakness or demagogy, to allow appropriations to exceed income. They differ only in degree from their fellows in all democratic regimes. With these reservations, inflation in France, like everywhere else, is a function of monetary and economic policy. From 1926 to

[2] Lüthy, p. 319.

1930 France experienced a period of progress and stability. Those in power from 1930 to 1935 even attached so much importance to a balanced budget and stable prices that the country was afflicted with a really unbearable deflation, to which the government of the Popular Front reacted overzealously. Inflation was again prevented in the years following 1952. All these developments, though they happened in France, are neither more nor less mysterious than anywhere else. There, as elsewhere, a few simple steps are enough to curb or release the monster.

The success achieved by the State, under the Monnet Plan favoring basic industry, is well known. Just after the war, faced with the cumulative ruin of the depression of 1930–39 and the years of the Occupation, the government courageously decided to concentrate public, if not private, resources in areas of basic industry (coal, electricity and gas, railroads, steel, oil, cement). The first three of these were nationalized, and the event gave currency to a legend: in France the initiative is taken by the State, and the nationalized sectors are models of modern progress. Certain circles in France, with the same propensity for creating myths, denounce the State-administered sector which functions at a loss or requires subsidy. The reality is simpler; from the moment when the State itself underwrote large investments in key industries, these industries had to take the lead in the work of reconstruction. Now here is what happens to this ordinary phenomenon: "France today possesses the industrial productive capacity of a modern country, but everywhere, as soon as production began to approach the level of consumption, it appeared to flag. A multitude of open sluice-gates seemed to be inserted between the magnificently equipped key industries and a stagnating market which drew off the increased social product and caused it to run dry before it reached the consumer. . ."[3] There is actually no such thing as these "open sluice-gates." The French distribution system is probably cumbersome and costly. It is obvious that it does not prevent the delivery of the product to the consumer

[3] Lüthy, p. 299.

if it is understood that in 1948-49, three to four years after the war
ended, the results of modernization were more apparent in the key
industries than in most of the others. Since then certain industries,
all privately owned (electrical engineering, machinery, electronics,
chemicals), have become at least as "magnificently equipped" as the
nationalized industries.

    "Five years have passed since the triumphant announcement in
the winter of 1948-49 that French industry had again reached the
maximum output in its history, that of 1929, and no further advance
has been reported; and if French production is stagnating about a
high point reached a quarter century ago, without any apparent
prospects of ever exceeding it, French wages are stagnating below
the depressed level of 1938." [4] Everything in this description is false
or falsified. Twice, a slowing up or cessation of expansion was noted
during the stages of the stabilization of prices (1949-50, 1952-53); in
the meantime, beginning with the second half of 1950 and up to
mid-1952, expansion had been swift even though affected by a rise
in prices. It was not until the second half of 1953 that a healthy
expansion, without inflation, began. If the whole of the elapsed
period is included, we see nowhere the insurmountable barrier set
up by the 1929 volume of production, which was reached around
1949 and greatly surpassed since then. As for the contradiction
between 1929 production and 1938 wages, it deceives the uninformed
reader. In 1938 the net rate of investment had become almost zero,
the hourly wage rate, artificially swollen by the forty-hour law, did
not correspond to the true possibilities of the economy. The distribution of wages in 1950 was quite different from that in 1938;
because the discrepancy between Paris and the provinces and between
men and women had been reduced and indirect pay ("fringe benefits") had gone up considerably, cost per hour for labor, which has
swiftly risen since 1950, was not abnormally low in relation to the
development of production.

    How often have we read, from the pens of foreign journalists,

[4] Lüthy, p. 299.

that French wages were low! What is the frame of reference? American wage rates? Then it is true French wages are low, but so are wages in all European countries. In comparison with European wages, they are not low. Higher than in Italy or Holland, certainly not as high as in Sweden or Switzerland, a little lower than in Great Britain, they have been somewhat better in buying power than in Germany and are still at least equal in that respect. We realize the complexity of such comparisons between real wages. Comparisons on the basis of official exchange rates probably overestimate the wages of French labor for the last few years because of the over-valuation of the franc. Wage earners do not spend their pay the same way in different countries: on the whole the French worker is not as well housed but is better fed than those across the Rhine. But it was a question here only of clearing up the myths. French wages are not abnormally low either in comparison with the national income or with the European average. On this subject we must resign ourselves; France resembles the other countries, not that unique and paradoxical being whose eccentricities observers are always lovingly or disparagingly emphasizing.

A few observations now on another legendary subject: taxation. To begin with, let us recall that France, in proportion to her national revenue, is more heavily taxed than the United States. According to M. Lauré's figures,[5] American tax rates, applied in France, would have yielded $4,972 million instead of the $8,295 million collected by the French system. American rates would have to be raised two thirds to equal the relative return of French tax rates.

But no one questions the burden of French taxes; what is doubted is the extent to which they are correctly paid. Anglo-Saxon honesty is supposed to be irreproachable, tax fraud in France rampant. Probably the antithesis has some truth in it, but I am afraid that the Anglo-Saxons do not quite earn such undue honor, nor the French such opprobrium.

[5] Maurice Lauré, *Traité de politique fiscale* (Paris, 1956), p. 198. The figures referred to are for 1953.

In all lands certain groups in society are especially inclined to fraud—peasants, tradesmen or small manufacturers, the self-employed, and lastly, certain members of the professions. The tendency toward fraud is first and foremost a function of the difficulty in auditing accounts, and this difficulty in turn is particularly manifest in the case of incomes which the Treasury calls "mixed": that is, which include both salary and profits. Categories composed of persons who are by nature and tradition individualists are spontaneously hostile to taxation in its modern form, which relies on exact reporting of economic activity and on discrimination between sources of income. Fraud on wages amounts to little in France, as elsewhere, because it is impossible. Salaries, here, represent a smaller part of national revenue, mixed income a more important portion (slightly over 30 per cent in France for private business or mixed incomes, compared to some 10 per cent in the United States). Tax evasion develops more serious consequences in France than elsewhere because the classes of people having the desire and the means for it are more numerous.

Among the taxpayers of the professions, doctors and surgeons have bad reputations just about everywhere. In the United States, 10 per cent of the taxpayers brought into court for tax evasion are doctors.[6] M. Lauré has made an interesting comparison between France and the United States on this particular point. He concludes that incomes declared, according to the schedule of rates, by members of the professions are analogous in the two countries, allowing for the difference of income levels. The number and importance of increased payments ordered by the internal revenue departments are analogous. In the $9,000–$10,000 bracket the audit in the United States affected 7 per cent of the declarations and led to the payment of increased sums in 25 per cent of the cases. In the $15,000–$20,000 bracket, the audit applied to 11 per cent of the declarations and occasioned addi-

[6] Lauré, p. 369. For technical reasons, incomes of doctors are now better known in France.

tional payments in 17 per cent of the cases.[7] These figures are of the same order as in France.

Our country nevertheless offers a few original traits in this matter. Farmers, on the whole, pay little in direct taxes, not because of evasion, but by virtue of the laws, and particularly the interpretation given them. It is true that a great many small farmers, proprietors, and tenant farmers would not be in a position, in any event, to pay substantial taxes, since their cash incomes scarcely exceed what is considered the minimum living wage in the cities. But the wealthy farmers—and there are some—are favored.

Since the revenue department has ways of knowing about investments in securities, the movement toward circumspect banks in Switzerland and the United States has become a means of tax evasion as well as a guarantee against currency devaluation. There is an underground circulation of capital. A proportion of gross income as well as of capital gains never appears in official returns, which are open to inspection by the examiners.

Whatever the amount of capital that has taken refuge abroad or is hidden inside France, and whatever the loss of receipts, each attributable to evasion, the French attitude toward taxation remains unique. Public opinion, which in the United States and Great Britain severely censures evasion—at least openly—affects an extraordinary indulgence in France. The contrast is a function of collective psychology: the British and Americans pride themselves, not without some hypocrisy, on good citizenship (the art of charging many more or less private expenditures to business expense accounts is not unknown on the other side of the Channel or across the Atlantic); Frenchmen boast of cynicism, and when they are honest— which happens oftener than is believed—they excuse themselves by invoking the wretched bondage of the wage earner. The French do not have a system of values corresponding to the socio-economic institutions they have created. No nation has progressed so far in

[7] Lauré, p. 370.

the methods of redistribution recommended by the theorists of the welfare state, yet no people have maintained as much spontaneous antipathy to State intervention, as much indulgence toward free-loaders. This inconsistency leads us from the consideration of myths to a closer look at reality.

*   *   *

What are the main characteristics of the economic development of France in the twentieth century?

An initial fact is furnished by the employment statistics. The numbers employed in industry (not including the building trades) remained about the same from 1906 to 1954: in 1906 there were 5,120,000 in 87 *départements,* and in 1954 the figure was 5,360,000 in 90 *départements.*[8] This steadiness was the result of movements in opposite directions. From 1921 to 1931 industrial employment increased by 900,000 and from 1936 to 1954 by more than a million (1,100,000), but it decreased by more than a million during the years of the depression. Industrial growth was due essentially to an increase in average productivity, itself the result partly of transfers of workers into branches or enterprises where productivity is higher, and partly of progress made in the original occupations themselves.

The slow pace of industrialization is all the more striking in that the agricultural manpower has decreased steadily: 54,000 a year from 1921 to 1929, 35,000 from 1926 to 1931, and 59,000 between 1946 and 1954.[9] Until just after the Second World War, public opinion con-

---

[8] Employment statistics are subject to dispute in matters of detail. The latest figures given in the National Institute of Statistics and Economic Studies, *Mouvement Économique en France, 1944 à 1957* (Paris, 1958), are the following: the active agricultural population went from 8.84 million in 1906 to 5.19 in 1954; the industrial population (including the building trade) went from 5.93 million in 87 *départements* in 1906 to 6.85 (90 *départements*) in 1954; those engaged in tertiary trades and services went from 4.74 million to 6.28 in this period.

[9] Agricultural population (in millions)

	Men	Women	Total
1901	5.48	3.28	8.76
1921	5	3	8
1936	4.22	2.53	6.75
1954	3.55	1.93	5.48

tinually deplored the rural exodus, when it should have been deploring the delay in industrial expansion.

The progress of agricultural production was slow during the first years of the century. During the last years of the nineteenth century, the vineyards had been attacked by phylloxera, and cereal producers had suffered the effects of price drops and disruption in the world market caused by American and Canadian grains. It took years for agriculture to recover the losses in men and investment caused by the First World War. From 1930 on, the world-wide depression brought other afflictions. It has been estimated that from 1901 to 1939 the value of production grew by some 10 per cent, while manpower was decreasing one third. On the other hand, progress sped up after the Second World War: between the 1934–38 average and 1955, manpower diminished by a fifth and production increased a third. Agriculture made more progress in ten years than during the preceding half-century.

It seems to me that these figures point out the major problem presented by the development of the French economy in the twentieth century: why did the workers who were leaving the rural areas not enter industry in greater number? Why did industry not experience a quantitative expansion as well as an increase in productivity?

Two kinds of reasons may be advanced which we shall call, resorting to the jargon of the economists, *conjunctural* and *structural*. During the 1919–29 period of reconstruction and expansion, industrial employment, production, and productivity increased normally, at a pace comparable to that in neighboring countries. The slowing up observed when the figures for 1955 are compared with those for 1903 or 1929 is attributable above all to the lost years—1914–18 and again 1930–45. Following this line of thinking we should look first for the causes of the decline in the decade before the Second World War. None of the characteristics of collective psychology or social organization so often offered as causes of economic stagnation can be considered decisive, since France and the French were no different between 1920 and 1930 than they were from 1930 to 1940, and because the stagnation appeared in the course of only one of the two periods. A constant fact cannot be the cause of an intermittent effect. Hence, national character is not directly responsible for the alternation of rapid progress and prolonged stagnation.

This supposition still does not explain the length of the periods of stagnation. Why did France not find the means that all the other European nations, each in its own way, finally discovered? Why did she pass from severe deflation, sacrificing the economy to the currency, into a period of wild inflation, forsaking the future for illusory benefits granted workers by complaisant authorities? It has not been shown that the politicians, the parliamentary regime, or ministerial instability were solely responsible; the spokesmen of big interests clung to the disastrous myth of monetary integrity to the end. Only a modification of the rate of exchange, putting an end to the overvaluation of the franc brought on by the devaluation of the pound and the dollar, would have restored a normal relation between wholesale prices and the cost of living and made it possible to avert the protracted decline of prices which brought hardship to the people and proved economically ineffective. With a few exceptions, the leaders of the nation—not just the political element—recommended right up to the investiture of Léon Blum a policy which was at once unpopular and ineffective.

This example is not without its lesson and does not conform to the mythological image of government leaders lacking courage and ever ready to yield to the wishes of the governed or to the claims of this or that group. I know very well that the watchword "Protect the Currency" was not without echo in a country which a few years earlier had suffered inflation. It was popular with an important segment of the middle class and the peasantry. This notwithstanding, had the leaders been clearsighted in their pursuit of popularity they would not have resorted, with an obstinacy worthy of a better cause, to a policy of deflation which, by infuriating the wage earners, led to the explosions of 1936. The characteristics of governmental action were *intellectual rigidity* and *failure to appreciate reality*. Everything took place as though it were more important to be right than to succeed, as though sticking to a formula or a theory prohibited action by the humble and indispensable method of trial and error.

Ignorance of the mechanism of deflation and devaluation played its part right up to the emergence of the Popular Front. Its effect was still greater afterwards. Léon Blum imagined that he could combine massive distribution of buying power and easing of credit with the preservation of parity of exchange. When he limited the working week to forty hours for most industries, labor was averaging more than forty-four; Léon Blum was stupefied when he heard this during the Riom trial.

Even should we accept the "conjunctural" explanation, we are faced with certain "structural facts." Public opinion and those directing affairs have and had but a mediocre knowledge of things economic; more certain of their convictions than of their information, they were capable of going to the extreme with a theory, laying the blame on reality if they failed.

The conjunctural explanation leads to the structure of the economy by still another way. The French would not so readily have accepted ten years of "technical and organizational stagnation" had they not been somewhat suspicious of modern civilization as incarnated in industry. The millions of unemployed in Great Britain and Germany confirmed them in their skepticism and inclined them not to make an effort to industrialize, but on the contrary, to fall back on the agrarian base of the nation. Immigration was stopped, hundreds of thousands of foreign workers left the country, and the exodus from rural areas slowed down. No one, or almost no one, called attention to the fact that the reaction to the crisis was adding to the delay in the nation's progress toward a modern civilization, a reaction which would have been impossible if the population had not been practically stabilized for decades. In an increasing population, the trades and services could not have absorbed the new workers.

As for other structural factors, let us merely mention some of them. Between the nineteenth and twentieth centuries French in-

dustry went through a geographical shift unequaled elsewhere in
Europe. Small industry, which at the middle of the nineteenth
century made France the most industrialized country on the Continent, proved more an obstacle than a stimulus to further growth.
The protection given to agriculture toward the end of the century
spared the peasants the pains of reconversion and modernization; it
also allowed them to cling to traditional practices which yielded
modest returns. France, it is true, did not have sources of power
comparable to the Ruhr, but above all she was lacking in the social
and human elements which should have taken the initiative in
industrialization. In a non-socialist regime it is the entrepreneurs
who are the mainspring of the movement, the soul of development.
France, during the half-century before 1914, had a surplus of capital,
in spite of a modest rate of saving, and made loans all over the world.
The rural exodus caused by the slow progress of agricultural productivity (the population did not increase; the urge to increase the
volume of production was weakened by the fear of overproduction)
caused workers who could have been put to work in industry to move
into the towns. France, which played an important part in the
initial development of some modern industries (automobiles, aviation), never experienced a fever of industrial construction like the
one in Germany during the last quarter of the century. The rate of
development increased in France, as elsewhere, at the beginning of
the twentieth century. The nation did not find fulfillment for its
dreams in works of concrete or metal; entrepreneurs, most of them,
were building up family businesses. The bourgeois dynasties were
not animated by a will for infinite power. They were building in an
orderly and moderate fashion.

*   *   *

The rate of growth in a given country depends on many factors,
one or another of which is emphasized according to the frame of
reference or comparison selected. When it was learned how to use
the low-grade minerals of Lorraine, the production of steel soared;

it tripled between 1901 and 1914. Although the relative slowness of economic growth in the second half of the last century seems also due to psychological and social causes, and although these causes continue to operate somewhat in this century, the fact remains that except for the disastrous 1930–45 phase, the French economy has progressed at the same rate as that of her neighbors in the twentieth century. The chief reason for the difference between the progress achieved by France and by Germany between 1901 or 1929 and 1955 is not a national anemia or chronic paralysis but the half-accidental prolongation and aggravation of a crisis.

How does the French economy look today as compared with Germany's or Great Britain's? First, and above all, France is less industrialized, both absolutely and relatively, than the United Kingdom or Western Germany. Taking 100 as an index for industrial production in France, the index for Germany stands at 137, for the United Kingdom at 168 (these figures refer to the year 1955). The difference is similar in vocational distribution. Out of 1000 persons, 126 are employed in industry in France, 180 in Germany, 197 in Great Britain. Taking the index of industrial employment in France as being 100, that for Germany is 143, and for Great Britain 156. Since differences among the French, German, and English indices of production and employment are analogous, it follows that productivity per worker is about the same in the three countries.

Here is annual productivity per worker in industry:[10] Sweden 141, Norway 137, Switzerland 112, Great Britain 106, France 100, Western Germany 96, Italy 77. These figures will surprise many readers for whom German efficiency and French inefficiency are articles of faith. They confirm the advancement of the small Nordic countries, the advantages they get from a high degree of specialization. Moreover, the relations among French, German, Belgian, Dutch, and Italian wage rates do not justify belief in inferiority of output for French industry taken as a whole.

As for agriculture, comparisons between countries are difficult,

[10] After François Walter, *Etude sur le développement économique de la France.*

and many comparisons which are used currently are in fact meaningless. Productivity per laborer is usually greater where the yield per acre is low (which is the case in the United States). An American farmer feeds four or five times more people than a French peasant, but he cultivates more land. On the other hand, a high yield per acre may be the equivalent of low productivity per worker. A country like Holland, whose population increases swiftly in a confined space, must compensate for the effects of the law of diminishing returns by making costly investments.

The most valid comparison would consider the basic concept of value added, even though in case of overpopulation it may be wise to consent to a lower average value added to feed more people per acre of land. But such a comparison is extremely difficult to make, because the cost of production for each type of agriculture or undertaking is not exactly known.

With these reservations in mind, where does French agriculture stand among the European agricultural systems? It certainly stands below Danish agriculture, which has an exceptionally high level of technology and where all the peasants get technical instruction. But it is not certain, if we refer to the value added, that Dutch agriculture is superior to the French, which would not, however, justify any special satisfaction: the French problem was incomparably simpler than the Dutch problem. On the land at present cultivated in France, five million workers could produce food for more than forty-five million people. If they do not produce more it does not follow that the French case is exceptional but quite the opposite, that different nations have acted according to different circumstances.[11]

There is no question that it would not be hard to do better. With available resources of land and manpower agriculture could provide exports or supply additional workers to expanding industry. It has often been remarked that French agriculture is extraordinarily heterogeneous.[12] In part, this diversity results from variations in region,

---

[11] These considerations are borrowed from the study made by François Walter.
[12] Variations are great in different regions both in terms of percentage of male manpower engaged in agriculture (more than 50 per cent in the agricultural *départe-*

climate, soil, traditions. Multiple crop farming, rooted in time-honored custom, is still practiced in many localities, and does not yield easily to the requirements for high productivity. It is in agriculture even more than in industry that the commonplace remarks about the "swarm of little anachronistic enterprises" and the immense differences in productivity contain a germ of truth.

Is the slowness to merge, by the same token as the relative slowness to industrialize and the diversity of agriculture, to be taken as one of the peculiar features of our economy? Many figures are cited on this, especially those on the distribution of workers according to the types and sizes of enterprises. According to a study by the National Institute of Statistics and Economic Studies, based on the 1954 census, 52.7 per cent of industrial enterprises belong to individuals, while 31 per cent are *entreprises artisanales,* 12.5 per cent are individual or stock partnerships, and 2.5 per cent are joint or limited-liability corporations. In trade, 84.5 per cent of the concerns are privately owned and operated. As to the distribution of the labor force, another figure is striking: 96 per cent of the enterprises employ less than 50 workers, 83 per cent less than 5. But the multiplicity of small businesses is found everywhere. The essential statistics have to do with the distribution of labor according to the size of the enterprise: 36.6 per cent of the wage earners work in factories hiring from 1 to 50, 36.1 per cent in those employing 51 to 500, 27.3 per cent in those employing more than 500 workers,[13] of which 9.7 per cent are in those employing from 500 to 1000, 13.2 per cent 1000 to 5000, and 4.4 per cent over 5000. In business trades 17.3 per cent are in firms employing more than 50 wage earners.

---

ments of Brittany, 15 per cent in the Département du Nord, and 32 and 33 per cent in the north central and Mediterranean regions) and in use of fertilizer per acre (taking the nationwide average as 100, the index for the north of France is 249, and for the southwest and southeast, 49 and 29 respectively); in production of milk per cow, the national average taken as 100, the northern index is 135, in Britanny 81, and in the southwest 80. The backward regions are also those where industry is almost totally lacking. Industrialization is in fact one of the favorable, if not necessary, conditions for the modernization of agriculture.

[13] The corresponding figures for the United States and Great Britain are 48 and 46 per cent respectively.

In several sectors (automobiles, chemicals, electricity) a few companies dominate the scene and manufacture most of the product. In the automobile and cycle industries 1 per cent of the plants (60) do 52.6 per cent of the business and pay 69 per cent of the wages. In electrical engineering 0.9 per cent of the companies carry on 66 per cent of the business and pay 67 per cent of the wages. In the building materials industry the figures are 0.3 per cent (19), 53 per cent and 47 per cent. Percentages of the same order are met with in smelting (1.1 per cent of the enterprises and 52 per cent of the volume), in public works (1.7 per cent of the contractors and 45 per cent of construction). Unconcentrated sectors are, for example, the building industry, in which only 47 of 186,000 firms do an annual business of over one billion francs and represent only 7 per cent of the trade volume; shoemaking, where large companies are only 7 out of 35,000, with 14 per cent of the national product. As a whole, firms doing a business of over a billion francs represent only 0.14 per cent of the total number; they realize 40.3 per cent of the total business and pay 46.2 per cent of the cost of labor.

The usual idea that France is still the nation of small business is, then, not false. But most of the modern economic sectors (automobiles, chemicals, electronics) in France, as elsewhere, are controlled by a small number of large firms. Besides, dispersion and concentration as such do not mean a great deal. It all depends on the nature of small firms, their relation to big companies or to each other. Small industries can prosper by specialization and small businesses by cooperation. It is quite likely that in many sectors there are still large numbers of firms which are too small and more or less unproductive. Sometimes these marginal enterprises are protected rather than opposed by the larger ones, which thus ensure extra profits by maintaining prices at levels desired by the former.

This relative slowness in concentration is attended by the survival of precapitalistic legal entities. In 1954 family firms and partnerships did a business of 7,610 billion francs as compared with 9,513 billion for stock companies, 2,512 billion for nationalized establishments, and

6,633 billion for limited stock companies (*sociétés à responsabilités limitées*). According to the national accounts, wage payments amount to 58.9 per cent of net national income, while net income from ownership and business allocated to individuals is 34.9 per cent (in 1957). Contrary to the current belief abroad, wages are not artificially kept low in France by a "reactionary" management. The wage level, as we have said, is abnormally low neither with respect to the national income, nor by comparison with the neighboring countries. In the accounts for the year 1957,[14] dividends and partnership shares represent 661 billion, interest 743 billion, a total of 1,404 billion for return on capital as against 7,192 billion paid for wages and salaries, 1,363 billion in social security paid by business firms, and 2,536 billion for social allowances, and finally, 3,488 billion in indirect taxes. Really, the peculiarity of the distribution of income in France (setting aside tax evasion and hidden capital) is the contrast between two phenomena: *the importance of individual enterprises and mixed income, and that of the social welfare budget and miscellaneous assistance payments.*

Let us look, for example, at the cost of doing business. For a total of interest paid of 397 billion francs and dividends of 562 billions, wages and salaries amount to 5,790 billion, and social security taxes, paid directly or indirectly, to 1,363 billion. Thus, we have 7,153 billion for labor cost against 959 billion making up the return on capital investment. On the other hand, the net income for private businesses was 4,552 billion francs. It was the comparison of these two figures—5,790 billion for labor cost, and 4,552 billion of net return for individual entrepreneurs—which was cited in the controversial arguments, the income for family firms being falsely assimilated with profits.

It is equally instructive to compare the total labor cost (5,790 billion francs) or gross fixed capital formation (2,675 billion)[15] with

---

[14] *Rapport sur les comptes de la nation de l'année 1957*, p. 179.
[15] Gross capital formation for the economy as a whole comes to 4,050 billion francs.

state allocations to the accounts of companies or individuals. Family allowances add up to 2,536 billion, health and welfare assistance to 532 billion, and various economic subventions to 1,369 billion. Thus, assistance and allowances represent a total of 3,068 billion francs, as against 5,790 billion francs labor cost for businesses and 7,192 billion francs in wages and salaries for the whole country. Expenditures for social security and welfare are, then, more than 40 per cent of the total of wages and salaries. If we agree that *capitalistic* is the correct term for the legal structure of stock companies and the separation of property and labor, and if, on the other hand, we agree to characterize as *socialistic* the redistribution of wages and incomes by the State and its intervention in the management of the economy, we may well say that *the French economy of today is at the same time less capitalistic and more socialistic than the economies of other European nations.*

What are the causes of this complex and, in one sense, paradoxical structure? The survival of small family businesses has many causes. The protection of agriculture has encouraged the farmer to procrastinate in adjusting to a modern economy; fiscal laws have often favored the small family workshop or small tradesman. The French seem to attach importance to independence, and at times to prefer it to higher income. Resistance by the agricultural sector and individually conducted commercial or industrial and mixed income groups expresses a characteristic of the national psychology just as it is the result of a policy adopted by governments under pressure from the electorate or grouped interests.

As for social legislation and economic intervention, they arise sometimes from popular demands which are taken up by politicians, and sometimes from administrative initiative.

It was in the national interest that the social security program was directed toward the struggle against the falling birth rate and that family allowances (originally started by Catholic employers) became one of its main provisions. It was to encourage rapid development in one or another branch of industry that the State granted investment subsidies or guaranteed loans to certain industries. Subsidies destined to lower the price of motor fuel to the farmer had as their goal the mechanization of farming methods. The purchase of raw materials (nickel, for instance) within the French Union at a figure higher than the international price obligates the State to underwrite French producers so that they will not be at a disadvantage in world trade. Time after time, the State is induced to grant new subsidies on the heels of the discontinuance of previous ones in order to avert, at a given moment, a price rise of a particular product lest the rise, reflected in wages and cost of living, cause a general increase in prices. It would be easy to cite numerous instances of this.

Other subventions fit neither into the framework of the development program nor into the needs of day-by-day management of affairs. They are in response to the demands of special groups. They make up the deficit in one or another public service. One example has acquired symbolic value: the Office de l'Alcool, which is concerned with alcohol and the joint problems of viniculture, beet growing, and wine and alcohol manufacture. As though to deride mankind and his long-term planning, successive crop failures created temporary shortages, even though surpluses were still deplored. So there appeared a fundamental and normal weakness in the agricultural program: a volume of production which in good years exceeds the domestic demand and does not meet it in bad years creates incessant difficulties with opposite repercussions unless the surplus is exportable and the shortage easily met. When wine is involved neither of these conditions is satisfied. If it is grain, one is, but not the other: the surplus is exportable, but at a loss.

Need we add once again that the French singularity is only one of degree? Nowhere in the Western world are agricultural prices left to the automatic operation of the market, nowhere is production regulated only by the producers' reaction to unregulated price changes. But it is true that the combination of so many producers, each asserting his independence, of so many bureaus, of so many guaranteed prices and subsidies, is unique. Frenchmen by the millions complain of State spending, from which nearly all of them benefit. Individualism and state socialism make a curious mixture, like precapitalism and socialism.

*   *   *

Somewhere between the prewar and postwar periods there occurred in France a psychological change which it is easier to record than to explain. The two symptoms of this change are the substantial increase in the birth rate, which has produced a draft-age group larger by some 200,000 than before the war,[16] and the will for expansion which now inspires producers, entrepreneurs, management, and workers alike. Between the 1930's and the 1950's the French changed their outlook on life.

The steady balance between agriculture and industry was long a part of the national philosophy, which is now in the process, at least in leading administrative, economic, and intellectual circles, of evolving toward a "progressive" view: growth, no longer stability, is the goal; rural migration is no longer deplored but welcomed and often even desired.[17] Of course, a few academicians have never lost their nostalgia for the handicrafts, and spokesmen of certain agricultural factions are forever recalling the greatness of the peasant, God's representative on earth, contrasting him with the wretchedness of the worker who turns a screw eight hours a day when he is not sunk in the solitude of unemployment. These complaints are rarely heard any more.

Despite wars waged abroad—Indochina, then North Africa— despite the alternating stabilization and·inflation which the governments could easily have prevented, the postwar period, or in other

---

[16] The theoretical rate of increase is 0.78; the number of births per 10,000 inhabitants was 184 in 1956 (in Great Britain this was 161), whereas it had been 149 in 1938. It is the reversal of the trend which is striking, rather than the birth rate itself, which is still relatively low. Mortality has decreased at the same time. Life expectancy went from 58.2 years in 1933–38 to 66.5 in 1951.

[17] The planning commission foresees and favors it.

words, the short term of the Fourth Republic, has been, from the economic and social point of view, a time of recovery first, and then of modernization. From 1949 to 1957, the gross national product rose 46 per cent, population between the ages of four and thirteen 37 per cent, farm output 24 per cent, production of chemicals 132 per cent, the number of private cars doubled, investment in housing rose 142 per cent, and production of private automobiles increased 285 per cent. This record is not above those of other European countries; it is lower in some instances than Western Germany's, but it shows—as if there were need for it—French postwar vitality. The Fourth Republic had a troubled but not unproductive life. It failed overseas, but not in the metropolis. With mistakes and omissions, and not without disorder, it started the country along the way to modern civilization.

But, economically, the short-term heritage left to the Fifth Republic by the Fourth was difficult. The deficit in foreign trade and the shortage of exchange threatened a major crisis. In 1955 accounts had almost balanced, were favorable if one considers "expenditures of foreign governments in France," which may, if preferred, be considered as covering normal receipts, although of a political origin, or, as it were, exceptional. (Normal or not, these sums are no less regular.) The important sums advanced by the United States to finance the war in Indochina served to reconstitute the reserves. Unfortunately, in 1956 and 1957 the Mollet government increased expenses enormously in the effort to pacify Algeria, and by social legislation at home, without entirely balancing these expenditures with additional income. To make matters worse, obsessed by the desire for stability, Mollet contrived to prevent price rises by playing the game of subvention. The business deficit, the flood of imports, the slowness of foreign sales, were the inevitable results of this inflationary policy. It became necessary, at the close of 1957, to ask the United States and our European partners for loans.

The foreign-exchange deficit may be compared to the depression in the 1930's and the obstinate support of the franc, in spite of the devaluation of the pound and the dollar. Present events offer, in fact, another example of the rationalist pursuit of a single thought characteristic of French behavior. From 1931 to 1936 the fixed idea was to save the franc, whereas the only way to save the economy at that time would have been to "lose," that is, to devalue, the franc. This time the fixation is less fatal, since the goal is to maintain industrial expansion at any price, or, to put it differently, to promote continued economic growth. No one questions the advantages of growth: what is at stake is the possibility of re-establishing the balance of foreign trade without slowing temporarily the development of production. The classical measures—tighter credit, lower State expenditures—influence total demand whether it affects imported or exportable products, or products of domestic manufacture and consumption. In other words, proposing to recover the balance of foreign trade, the classical measures also suppress goods and services which would have had little influence on the foreign trade balance.

Based on this irreproachable reasoning, certain bureaucrats supplied politicians with the argument with which they justified the refusal of a deflationary policy and exhausted the monetary reserves before taking restrictive measures. It is obviously preferable not to sacrifice expansion on the altar of equilibrium, but to recover the balance in foreign trade without slowing the increase of economic growth. The whole thing is to know whether this desirable goal is accessible. As so often in connection with French policy, the question must be asked: is it possible?

The battle against inflation was not undertaken seriously until the fall of 1957. By the summer of 1958, domestic prices were generally stabilized. Under the favorable impetus of General de Gaulle, a repatriation of some gold and evacuated capital took place. The danger of a crisis in foreign exchange was for the time being averted. But the essential thing was yet to be done: that is, to put the French economy in a position to enter the European Common Market.

During the closing days of 1958, General de Gaulle's government published a combination of economic, fiscal, and financial measures which at certain points continued the preceding attempts, at others inaugurated a new policy. The reduction of the impasse—that is, of the discrepancy between State expenditures and revenues—to less than 600 billion francs was the repetition of what had been done the year before. Investment allocations were higher than the deficit. The normal budget—"above the line," as the English put it—was in surplus.

The 15 per cent devaluation of the franc was also a liquidation of the past. Since the inflation of 1950-51, French currency had been regularly overvalued and the artificial rate had been maintained by means of a combination of administrative expedients (tax on imports, subvention of exports). The devaluation of 1957-58 had not restored the balance because it had been done in a moment of crisis and because later price rises had quickly recreated the disparity (which was relatively small, however, at the end of 1958).

The originality of the policy chosen by General de Gaulle and M. Pinay lies neither in the reduction of the impasse nor in the monetary adjustment, but in the means adopted to increase receipts and prevent the rise of prices. The elimination of some 200 billion francs in subsidies, the fixing of the percentage of liberated import at 90 per cent: these two measures are the symbol of a break with the protectionism and government intervention which were characteristic of the past. The purpose is to restore a healthy currency and realistic prices—two conditions indispensable for the consolidation of the remarkable progress achieved since the war.

The 1959 budget imposes national sacrifices made inevitable by the circumstances. In 1955-56, wages increased faster than productivity. Civil and military expenses in Africa and Europe cannot fail to be expressed as a lessening of consumers' income. General de Gaulle's government has had the good sense to realize the consequences of its economic program, and intends to provide itself with the means to carry forward the tasks it has set itself, and which the electorate has apparently approved.

The choice of methods may be surprising. The Gaullists and the General himself had always declared hostility to the Little Europe of the six-nation Common Market: once again the King of France was forgetting the quarrels of the Duke of Orléans, and a party, passing from the opposition into power, was changing its language. The liberal spirit of the economic reforms of 1958 could not be anticipated either, but the initiative came from the Committee of Experts and the Minister of Finance, not from the Union for the New Republic. General de Gaulle let himself be convinced that the restoration of a healthy currency was absolutely necessary for all the rest—economic progress, the Common Market, the coherence of the French Community, the pacification of Algeria. Once the objective was accepted, he made all the needed decisions however unpopular they might be, with a determination lacked by his predecessors. But the problem of the trade balance is not, on that account, solved.

On paper, France should have less trouble balancing its foreign exchange than Great Britain and Germany: the fact is that she raises her own food, while British and German imports necessarily entail a considerable sum destined for the purchase of food products. Foreign trade does not represent a high proportion of the national product. Compared with a gross national product, at market prices, of 20,520 billion francs in 1957, French importation of goods (cost, insurance, and freight) was 1,726 billion, exports 1,234 billion, totaling 2,960 billion francs in foreign trade, or 14.5 per cent of gross national product (at market prices).

The large deficits in 1956 and 1957 were ascribable to three causes: the budgetary deficit, which in France, as everywhere, is automatically expressed as foreign deficit; subsidiarily, the bad weather conditions during the winter of 1957 (although the balance in exchange of foodstuff was in surplus by 34 billion francs in 1955, it was unfavorable by 70 billion in 1956, balanced in 1957); and lastly, political developments, the Suez expedition and the war in Algeria.

The Suez expedition caused a sudden temporary rise in freight rates, forcing transfer of certain oil purchases to the dollar zone.

Accounts for the first half of 1957 were affected by these accidents to the amount of about 50 billion francs. As to the war in Algeria, it is not easy to estimate its effect on the balance of payments exactly. Government consumption of machinery went from 341 billion to 428 and 504 billion francs in 1956 and 1957, while exports of the same products, amounting to 467 billion in 1955, made little improvement (450 billion in 1956, 503 in 1957). One may well think that exports of these products would have made better progress if the State had not increased its own buying. About 40 billion francs were spent purchasing military supplies abroad during those same two years. The mobilization of a few hundred thousand men reduced the labor force and added to inflationary pressure. France's total expenses in Algeria probably amounted to some 700 billion francs in 1957, but part—perhaps half of this—represents a transfer rather than an addition: what is spent in Algeria is what would have been spent on maintaining divisions for NATO. Whatever the cost of war in Algeria may be, it has been only one of the causes of the inflation responsible for the deficit in foreign trade. Inflation itself was due above all to bad management of public finances. But it would be wrong to believe that with a strong and stable government all obstacles will be easily overcome.

In one respect, industrialization adds to the difficulties. France does not have in her own soil most of the raw materials needed for industry. In order to increase the output of coal by a few million tons a year, capital investment which in the long run would not be profitable would have to be made. Expansion requires not only additional importation of raw materials but also of equipment (between 1954 and 1957, imports of machinery almost doubled in value, reaching a total of 250 billion francs in 1957). The balance of trade will be restored only on condition that industry succeed in selling abroad a growing percentage of the annual surplus of production.

Of course, there is no reason why French industry should not under normal conditions gradually expand its foreign outlets. During the past few years, the pilot industries (chemicals, engineering, automobiles, electricity, and electronics) have shown no less improvement abroad than at home. The fact still remains that at the present time only one sector of the economy is directed at exporting, and it, aside from price conditions, requires a business and banking organization and a state of mind which do not appear overnight.

For the time being, the make-up of French exports characterizes a half-industrialized country. Food products make up 16.7 per cent of the whole, raw materials and half-finished products 44 per cent, manufactured products 39.2 per cent. This last figure is increasing, but it is still relatively low. This half-industrialized country is now assuming heavy responsibilities in Africa, quite apart from the war in Algeria.

The zone of the franc, which some day, thanks to the oil of the Sahara, will perhaps improve the foreign trade balance of the French mainland, is for the time being a burden. It absorbs investment capital in a quantity not to be ignored (100 to 150 billion francs, not including Algeria), and reduces the sum available for investments at home. It absorbs, especially, finished products representing some 45 per cent of the value of finished goods exported. In order to justify a certain overseas policy the press often emphasizes the value of colonial territories as customers of the homeland. If the goal were to gain buyers at any price the reasoning would be sound. But the manufactured goods and vehicles sold in Africa could probably have been sold to countries which had strong currencies or which were suppliers of raw materials. French Africa is currently selling to Metropolitan France 75 per cent of her farm produce and receives nearly 60 per cent of her industrial finished products from France.

Thus is stated the problem of the coming years. From 1953 to 1957 everything was sacrificed to expansion. Industrial production increased 10 per cent a year, but from 1956 on inflation caused the loss of reserves built up by American aid. The restrictive policy adopted in 1957 has put an end to the rise of prices and reduced the unfavorable balance of trade. France has been able to spend some 1,000 billion francs in Africa and to continue modernizing her economic structure, but inflation has resulted. She can continue her spending in Africa and put an end to inflation, but will the expansion not be paralyzed, or at least slowed down?

Government advisors answer this question with a wager. If confidence in the franc is revived and if Frenchmen repatriate the capital they have sent abroad, foreigners will come to make capital investments in France and in the Sahara. The stability of the new currency will bring about a reversal of the movement of capital and this will permit a frontal attack on industrialization in Europe, the pacification of Algeria, and the development of the territories of the Community in Africa. Repetition of the "Poincaré miracle" is possible, the experts insist. If peace were restored in Africa, certainly. The answer is more difficult if we assume that the conflict is to be prolonged.

*   *   *

According to a myth quite widespread in the United States, the French economy is an Augean stable waiting for its Hercules. In 1954, Mendès-France was hailed as the long-awaited hero. In fact, at the time of his investiture, he appointed a commission of nine members, composed of civil servants, charged with suggesting necessary reforms. He had no ready-made plan, because the French economy does not in fact lend itself to such a plan.

The commission of experts named by Pinay suggested most of the measures adopted by General de Gaulle's government at the end of 1958. These measures give a precise idea of the reforms required by the economy. We have already taken note of the enormous total of the appropriations and interventions by which the State for one reason or another reduced the price of a commodity or service. The elimination of 200 billion francs in subsidies is a step in the right direction. In the same way, reducing the tax rates on value added to four shows the type of reform, leading above all to simplification, needed by the French fiscal system. The restoration of the currency

by a liberal method is the equivalent of what took place a few years
ago in most European countries. In spite of everything, if we leave
aside the crisis in foreign finance, the outstanding fact of the period
since the war is the progress made in French economic affairs,
especially in technical progress in industry, but also in agriculture,
the general determination to build and revive. Whether it finds its
Hercules or not, the French economy is in full transformation and,
barring extreme political unreason, can look forward to a prosperous
future.

Of course, all is not for the best in the best of worlds; there are
still areas of darkness. The first is in the field of construction. The
population has acquired the habit of not budgeting a normal part
of income for housing. The deterioration of dwelling quarters has
been the outcome of this bad judgment and those renting furnished
lodgings pay too much because the well-housed do not pay enough.
The number of units completed in 1957 rose to 274,000, whereas
about 50,000 more should have been built. One sector of the building industry has also been modernized; some public-works projects
and the experiments in industrial prefabrication are in the forefront
of progress. But another sector is still composed of a horde of pygmy
contractors working for private or semipublic organizations, too
numerous, and putting up too many different types of apartments.
In six months, General de Gaulle's ministry has effected a few of
the necessary reforms (a substantial rise in rent rates, apartment
house building associations, a beginning of the reform of real estate
legislation, and so on). In a few years the heritage of a long period
of demagogy will be on the way to liquidation.

The second zone of shadow is in agriculture. Not that the outlook
is unfavorable. On the contrary, it is easy to imagine exceptional
prosperity some ten years from now. In the abstract everyone is in
agreement on the objectives: to limit the production of grain, whose
surplus is exportable only at a loss, and to increase animal stock,
meat, and dairy products, for which demand is increasing as the
living standard rises, and whose prices make foreign sales possible.
The change in the relative prices of vegetables and meat products

provided for in the 1957 laws is threatened with delay or prevention by the activity of pressure groups. Producers of grain and beets are especially powerful, and the big operators are in a position to carry the little ones with them in their demands and protests. Government leaders are themselves caught between the desire to make the market price of meat profitable to encourage the farmers to produce more of it, and the fear of provoking a price rise motivated by the psychological significance of the price of beefsteak. Migration from rural areas, in itself desirable, threatens to empty the countryside of the labor needed for stock production.

More generally, the discrepancy between agricultural production in the various regions should be gradually cut down: areas without industry, with small and traditionally operated farms, devoted to multiple crop farming, are inefficient. Modernization can be achieved only by the spread of agricultural education, the consolidation of parcels of land, and, often, too, the specialization of crops. Once again, a long and exacting task.

Abroad, the most cited zones of darkness are alcohol and fiscal injustice. France has been for centuries a wine-producing and consuming country: Frenchmen of all classes have a tendency to drink beyond the limit set by doctors and public-health authorities. The right granted to producers to distill a certain quantity of alcohol themselves seems to have unfortunate effects on health in some regions. In addition, the Office de l'Alcool, obliged to buy beets, cider, or surplus wine, costs the Treasury considerable amounts in some years. No doubt, measures aimed at a reduction of the consumption of wine, and especially of spirituous liquors, would be taken by a benevolent and all-powerful government. But the insistence by millions of voters on the rights of home distillers is also a fact which a democratic regime cannot overlook. As to the surpluses of the Office de l'Alcool, they can and should be reabsorbed (they have been recently). But do American authorities always manage to keep crops whose price is guaranteed from exceeding the demands of the market?

As for *the* tax reform, ardently desired by everyone, it is not

achieved for the simple reason that there can be no such thing. Our
tax system is not without flaw, but it is not essentially different from
those of other Western countries. Indirect taxes might be differently
distributed; the rise in taxes on wine, alcohol, and tobacco (which
M. Pinay has just settled upon) corresponds to the ideas of most
public-health authorities and "enlightened despots." If the proportion
of direct taxes is lower than in Great Britain and the United States
the causes are, in part, not legislative: they include lower per-capita
income, a volume of mixed income partially evading taxation, the
amount reserved in advance for administrative expense, and the
importance of tax evasion. The defects in the French revenue laws
result from improper interference by legislators who, by dint of
exemptions and amendments, end by compromising the best conceived tax measures, such as the tax on value added.

The present difficulties are those of an expanding economy, some
of them created by deep-rooted custom or threatened interests, others
by growth itself. Consolidation, agricultural specialization, and reconversion are delayed by the normal tendency of producers, especially farmers, to keep to their accustomed way of living and
working. Growth itself stirs up dissatisfaction and, occasionally,
revolt.

Public-opinion polls in France reveal an astonishing, almost infinite
capacity to be uninformed about favorable events. Many workers,
when questioned, say there has been no change, although their real
income has gone up 5 per cent a year. Hostility to the regime on the
part of half the working class, as expressed by the vote for the
Communist Party, may have originally been provoked by slow progress or the isolation of factory workers in a predominantly peasant
nation, but it has now become crystallized in institutions and a sort
of traditional attitude: one votes *for* the party which is *against*.

Lastly, growth is more painful than usual when it takes place in
a country with a static population. Between 1954 and 1957 all categories of consumption increased. But within each category, the rise
in income could involve a decrease, in absolute value, of buying

power devoted to the purchase of a given item (grain, for example). Now growth is the more readily accepted when changing percentages necessitate no decrease in absolute value. This condition, apparently met when only the various categories of consumption, or even the different branches of industry (all moved forward from 1949 to 1957) are observed, is not fulfilled if we are referring to local areas. The acceleration of the birth rate does not change the general direction of development: the gap between rich and poor *départements* is widened. The former, industrialized, are the ones to profit most by modernization. The others, with a few exceptions, remain deserted and tend toward an irremediable decline. Forty-five million Frenchmen could easily earn their bread from the fertile land alone and concentrate in the industrial centers. In other words, growth had not disarmed the age-old hostility of the working class and it stirred up a spirit of protest in areas threatened with depopulation.

The outlook for the coming years is for an acceleration in development on the sole condition of political stability. The postwar generation will be flooding the labor market in another three years. France will be destined either for unbearable social tensions, or for expansion. Unless the war in Algeria paralyzes the nation, the chances for prosperity seem to me to outweigh the risk of crisis.

*   *   *

This comparatively optimistic analysis will, I fear, run into some skepticism. A stagnant economy, low wages, reactionary management, low industrial potential—all these assertions are no longer questioned. French pressure groups are famous all over the world— as though other countries had none. The structure of the agricultural market and the surpluses created by price supports are examined under a magnifying glass, as if those phenomena were unknown in the model countries on the other side of the Channel and the Atlantic. People talk as though, in our century, France had remained on the fringe of modern civilization, and the French engineers had not contributed to the development of the automobile and aviation.

They pretend to be unaware of the fact that France is at the fore-front in some technical fields (aluminum, cement, electronics, water power, dynamos), or that in others she holds an honorable position. The most incontrovertible figures on the relations between wages and productivity on the two sides of the Rhine are ignored or taken with skepticism. Once and for all, French cities must be judged by their slums (which admittedly are too numerous); French trade must be symbolized by the survival of *Les Halles* in the center of Paris; industry must be in the image of the handicraft sector. When the existence of a modernized sector is conceded—and this is now the fashion—that is what must be considered abnormal.

I shall not end on a note of smug optimism. The French economy was making progress when it was ravaged by the disaster of the 1930's and the war; events in Africa pose the threat of another catastrophe. Even if we had done as well as our neighbors—which has not always been the case—we should have no reason to boast, for in many respects we are more fortunate. It is true that when coal was almost the only source of energy, we lacked an essential playing card. But we have available more space and richer soil than does West Germany or Great Britain. It is easier to supply a livelihood, and a good one, to 45,000,000 Frenchmen on 213,000 square miles than for 50,000,000 Germans to live on 95,000 square miles, or 50,000,000 Englishmen on 94,000 square miles.

It is also true that the French psychology and political system have made their imprint on the economy of the country. The economic systems of other European countries, perhaps due to an optical illusion, do not seem so "national." The combination of precapitalism and socialism seems to reflect both the Frenchman's taste for personal independence and his constant recourse to the State. The bureaucrats organize and modernize; politicians protect their constituents singly or in groups. Public opinion, eager for progress, is imbued with the idea of vast investments, but limiting consumption in favor of investment is not readily accepted. The desire to bolster the old building is no less keen than the dream of building everything new.

The dialectic of conservatism and revolution does not spare the economy. Customary ways of thought and family traditions are not, and refuse to be, adapted to a technical civilization. The subordination of everything to productive efficiency and quantity—these demands of modern industry have not been approved, even by the elite. It is in France that one is accused of having the soul of a shopkeeper or of being a slave of capitalistic interests when one figures the cost of integrating 9,000,000 Algerians. It is in France that political parties like to conceal the interests they defend behind ideologies. Crude oil exercises a true attraction only on condition that it be buried under burning sands. The romance of the desert inspires explorers more than the economics of a strong currency does.

With all these things noted, what strikes one is the fundamental similarity—aside from a few retarded sectors—between the progress of the French economy and that of other European economies, a similarity which has become accentuated since 1945, after having disappeared between 1930 and 1939. In the decade before the war, each country chose its own fate, and France's choice, through a series of accidents, was catastrophic. For the rest of the time, the style and pace of the movement vary, but not the main features. "We control Nature only by obeying her." One can command technical civilization only on condition of acceptance of its laws and benefits in order to limit its ravages.

The final question of the historical destiny of France is always the same: how shall people who rationalize their dreams and conceal their disabilities from themselves arrive at a recognition of reality and adapt themselves to it?

IV ❧

TRAGEDY OF AN EMPIRE

THE war in Indochina lasted nearly eight years: begun in December 1946, it came to an end in July 1954 with the armistice of Geneva, which sanctioned the partition of the country into two states, North Vietnam, under a Communist government, and South Vietnam, with a government composed of nationalists and anti-Communists, influenced and aided by America. The Algerian rebellion was started in November 1954 by the secret branch for military action of the M.T.L.D. (*Mouvement pour le Triomphe des Libertés Démocratiques*), which later became the *Front National de Libération* (F.L.N.). In the fall of 1958, the rebellion was still not quelled. It is not likely that this sort of war can end within the near future unless agreement is reached between the French government and the F.L.N.

Historically, the twelve years of the Fourth Republic seem to have been dominated by these two conflicts, which may be called colonial but whose magnitude made them national. In order to maintain herself in Indochina France committed more military strength than had been needed to establish herself there. Never at any time in the past had she sent overseas an army as large as the one which is attempting to bring the task of pacification in Algeria to a successful conclusion. The attempt not to lose costs more in the twentieth century than the effort to win did a hundred years ago.

This fact—and many others which we shall have occasion to note as we go along—has convinced the mass of public opinion in the

United States and Great Britain that the best—the only—policy available to ex-colonial powers is to organize their retreat in such a way as to safeguard their interests, both economic and cultural, after giving up their sovereignty. Such was the policy adopted in Asia by Great Britain (the independence of India, Burma, Ceylon, and more recently, of Malaya), and also by Holland under joint pressure from the United States and the Soviet Union. Such was not France's policy in Indochina and North Africa. Such is the policy finally instituted in the French African territories south of the Sahara.

Why did France insist on maintaining her rule or her presence by methods which had been condemned by world opinion and whose failure was confirmed by experience?

* * *

"Athenians of the modern age," the French are often called. Have they behaved like the Athenians after the Peloponnesian War?

The Athenians at least had an excuse: the one possessed by people who have nothing left and who, having lost everything, are concerned only with the reconquest of it. The French, who had recovered everything, ought to have applied all their intelligence to safeguarding the future of this astonishingly preserved treasure. They have not done so. When the first uprisings took place in Madagascar, in Indochina, it was military reflexes that came into play and not the precepts of political wisdom: the French dreamed only of sending troops and making gun-powder talk, forever putting off until later the need to examine the substance of the problem and to go ahead with the needed reforms. "Hasten to take up arms, man the triremes" was already the word in the time of Isocrates, who reproved Athenian politicians for the only response they had to the insurrections of the moment . . . At the beginning there is a military defeat from which both countries recovered but which deeply affected their destiny. This defeat was followed in both cases by the accession to power of a reactionary and authoritarian oligarchy supported by the foreign conqueror. The government of the Thirty makes a pair with that of Vichy. Both show the same yearning for tradition, the same eagerness to sermonize the nation, to take as a text the misfortunes of the fatherland, feigning to look on them as the fatal consequence of a contemptible political system. . . The spectacle presented by Athens at this critical moment of her history rather resembles the one we now present to the world: superhuman military effort to which all else is subordinated (the 380 triremes and the large mercenary armies equipped by the Athenian State about 357–356 B.C. to fight the rebels of Samos, Rhodes and Chios correspond to the five hundred thousand men of our Algerian expeditionary forces; and the daring presence of Chabrias about 385–383 B.C. to checkmate Persian power equals our naval expedition to Egypt). Exorbitant expense unbalancing an always heavily burdened budget which is to be balanced by taxes which fail to touch clever tax-dodgers—a grave alienation of national independence resulting from the imperious needs of the Treasury, obliging the Athenian leaders to beg at times from the Great King for the loans today requested from the United States—diplomatic complications arising from aid given by the foreigner to the rebelling forces (Mausolus, satrap of Caria, behaves proportionately in the same way toward the people of Rhodes and Chios as does Colonel Nasser toward the leaders of the Algerian insurrection) . . . in a general way, vehement enmity between the advocates of war, who dream only of forceful action, eager to rejoice at the slightest successes, which they immediately transform into victories, and partisans of peace, exhorting their compatriots to negotiate and to devote to the commercial and industrial prosperity of Africa, which has become the tradesman's rendezvous, the wealth wasted in a vain struggle.[1]

The insistence on "hanging on" at any cost is not to be blamed in France only on the social class responsible for "collaboration": those who had been leaders and spokesmen of the Resistance, inspired by a sense of grandeur and passionately desirous of preserving the heritage, ended by losing it amid new disasters.

Unfortunately the question of empire arose just after the liberation of metropolitan France, even before the war against Germany was over. Indochina had had a special fate. It had remained under a French administration which obeyed the orders of the Vichy government. The Governor General, Admiral Decoux, was at heart faithful to Marshal Pétain, and he introduced a few ideas and organizations inspired by the regime of national revolution (the Vietnamese youth who were forced to march in parades were soon to discover Viet-

---

[1] Louis Harmand, in an article in *Le Monde*.

namese patriotism behind French patriotism and the cult of the Marshal). At the level of diplomacy Admiral Decoux was behaving in the only way possible. He had no means of keeping the Japanese from using the naval and air bases. The United States and Great Britain were in no position in 1940 to give help to the really ridiculously small forces the French authorities had at their disposal. By accepting a collaboration which the Japanese could have effortlessly imposed, the government of Indochina, following instructions from Vichy, did no harm to the Allied cause and kept alive future opportunities.

The war of the wave-lengths between Vichyists and Gaullists raged also in Asia. Admiral Decoux, adopting the slogans and sometimes the practices of Vichy, and the Gaullists, tracked down by the Admiral's police force, denouncing "collaboration" from abroad, prolonged French quarrels in radically different surroundings. After General de Gaulle's arrival in Paris the secret organization moved into the interior of Indochina and the French radio redoubled its vigor in opposition to the Admiral. In the army and the administration the number of *résistants* sincerely wanting to fight the Japanese or simply eager to clear themselves increased sharply. The Japanese replied to this resistance with the armed attack of March 9, 1945.[2] Not only had the French been unable to prevent the occupation, but they were publicly humiliated by the Nipponese soldiers. In the eyes of the Vietnamese, that day the French lost their claim to sovereignty (*le mandat du ciel*) forever.

The expeditionary corps, originally destined to take part in the final campaign against Japan, received orders to re-establish French rule in Indochina. It succeeded, not without fighting, in the south (Cochin China was legally a colony). In the north General Leclerc prepared a landing by agreement with the Chinese generals commanding the forces of occupation and with Ho Chi Minh, an old communist militant who was president of the Viet Minh govern-

---

[2] It is possible that the Japanese would not have tolerated the French administration up to the end even if the *résistants* had remained passive.

ment, established in Tonkin after the Japanese surrender. All during the year 1946 the outcome remained uncertain. General Leclerc had come back from Indochina convinced that reconquest would take an army of 500,000 men and long years of fighting. The governor named by General de Gaulle, Admiral Thierry d'Argenlieu, a naval officer who had become a monk, took the step of holding a conference at Dalat with policy leaders from the south, while Ho Chi Minh was negotiating in Paris. The latter returned to Hanoi without having obtained anything. After numerous incidents, the most serious of which was the bombardment of Haiphong by the French artillery, the Viet Minh started hostilities on December 19, 1946. The surprise blow, aimed at the massacre of the Hanoi garrison, failed. The war began with the French winning in the towns and the Viet Minh taking refuge in outlying districts or in concealment. All during 1947, the Socialist Moutet, minister for colonial affairs, kept throwing away the last chances for a peaceful settlement. Beginning in 1948 events followed their inevitable course.

One finds from the start not a resolute decision to fight but a state of indecision leading to war, the same sort of situation that was to occur so many times in the next few years. In Paris there was a divided government in which the advocates of the *résistance* regularly had the last word. On the scene there was a proconsul who acted on his own (the Dalat conference, the Haiphong shelling) beyond or contrary to instructions received from France. Once indecision and unauthorized acts together had brought on the explosion, the official slogan became "hold on" (just as at Verdun). Continuation of war was, indeed, in Paris the politically simple solution.

Indochina was not a colony for settlers. Aside from civil servants and the military forces, there were only a few thousand tradesmen, engineers, clerks, planters, and so on. Eventual independence involved no serious problems of transfer of population. The only argument against withdrawal—but it did have weight—was that the Viet Minh leaders were Communists. To negotiate with Ho Chi

Minh was to deliver Indochina to Communism. I doubt, though, that this was the only cause for the politicians' reluctance to give up. If the war's sole objective had been to raise a barrier against Communist expansion, the French government should have mobilized non-Communist nationalist strength, and promised to give others what it denied to Ho Chi Minh. It made a vague gesture in this direction when brought to bay by circumstances, but with what delay, what an art of giving and at the same time keeping back! In vast majority, the French officials, both civil and military, neither conceived of nor admitted the possibility of a war like the one the British carried on for years against the Communist guerrilla force and ended by granting independence to Malaya. The civil officials in Indochina had no future prospects in an independent Vietnam, and most of the policy-makers of both right and left, including some who had heroically opposed the Germans, refused to take the British Commonwealth as a model for the French Union. The mutation of the Empire was not to go forward by way of the independence of the overseas territories.

If Ho Chi Minh's Communism was not the sole or probably the chief cause of the outbreak of the conflict, it was the basis of the increased activity of 1950. In 1945, American authorities, in accord with the thinking and instructions of Roosevelt, were hostile to the return of the French to Indochina. In 1950, when the North Korean armies had crossed the Thirty-eighth Parallel, everything was suddenly reversed. Ho Chi Minh was no longer the hero of a battle against colonialism; he became a leader of a party playing the game of Soviet imperialism. The war in Indochina, which spokesmen for the French government had taken such pains to "sell" to the American administration, was taken over by the latter almost with enthusiasm when the intervention in Korea was decided upon. From then on the war continued to be costly in francs, but it brought in dollars. In 1953 the armistice in Korea opened a new phase. For the last time an opportunity to get out of the hornets' nest with honor was offered: instead of urging the Americans to link the

armistice in Korea with one in Indochina, Bidault continued to aim
for victory, whereas the United States was content with a draw.
The 1954 armistice was no different, in its territorial provisions, from
the one that could have been signed in 1953, but it followed the
defeat at Dien Bien Phu, which could not fail to have repercussions
over the whole world, especially in North Africa where the old
order was in danger.

Neither in Tunisia nor in Morocco, the two protectorates which
gained their independence in 1955-56, was nationalism involved
with Communism as it was at Tonkin. The party which led the
struggle in Tunisia, the Neo-Destour, was anti-Communist and pro-
West. In Morocco, the Istiqlal was led by bourgeois elements strongly
opposed to all social revolution. But under the cover of the protectorate there had been created a state of joint sovereignty which
Tunisian and Moroccan nationalists refused to admit and which
could not be modified without aiming a blow at what the Frenchmen in those two countries considered their rights. The spokesmen
for these settlers claimed that domestic autonomy would lead
rapidly to independence—and they were right—that independence,
in turn, would compel many of them to leave—and again they were
right. So they were stubbornly opposed to all reforms, including
reforms which would not have gravely compromised their position,
because they suspected (with good reason) an evolution toward
domestic autonomy and independence behind any concessions to the
nationalists. This intransigent conservatism, however understandable, determined the course taken by events: the *status quo* maintained to the end, then overnight, in July 1954 in Tunis, and in
September 1955 in Morocco, a complete reversal of policy, and, in
a few days or months, total independence for the protectorates.

What were the "French colonies" in North Africa? In Tunisia
in 1954 there were 270,000 Europeans and 3,500,000 Moslems; in
Morocco, 360,000 versus 7,640,000.[3] This number of Frenchmen,

---

[3] In the French zone.

about 5 per cent in Morocco and 7.5 per cent in Tunisia, is not large, but numbers alone do not measure importance.

In Morocco the French played an important part in agriculture: occupying 7 per cent of the arable land (a million hectares out of fifteen million), they realized 30 per cent of the value of plant production (28.5 billion francs out of 95 billion) and 5 per cent of stock production (5 billion out of 100) or 17 per cent of a sector providing 40 per cent of the national revenue. In the commercial and industrial domain covering the remaining 60 per cent of the national income, the Frenchmen's share represented a very large majority, reaching about 80 per cent, as opposed to 5 per cent for Moroccan industry (that is, moreover, the proportional Moroccan contribution to companies with capital of over 100 million francs), and 15 per cent for tradesmen and traditional craftsmen.[4]

The French colony had created a modern sector which included part of the Moroccan population, 25,000 civil servants, 60,000 farm laborers, 100,000 factory workers, 150,000 former soldiers, in all about 1.5 million people, or a fifth of the Moslem population. But the personnel of the groups in authority in the modern sectors was almost entirely French. Out of 5,500 employees of the higher rank of Neo-Sherifian ministries there were 165 Moroccans. The country had 875 French and 36 Moroccan doctors (of whom 17 were Jewish), and several hundred French and about thirty Moroccan engineers.

The French protectorates in Tunisia and Morocco had led to the immigration of three sorts of Frenchmen or Europeans: *government employees,* the *key personnel* of a modern industrial economy, and *settlers* in the strict sense: that is, landowners. Whatever the contribution of the first and third of these groups to the development of the country, foreigners occupying government posts and assuring for themselves the ownership of the soil have always, throughout history, stirred peoples to revolt. Those whom the French authorities

---

[4] These figures are taken from a study by M. de la Bastide d'Hust, "Lignes de force du Maroc moderne," in *Politique étrangère,* 1955.

had called in or whose coming they had favored, oftentimes in order to consolidate the French presence, became the chief obstacle to "decolonization." Rereading the history of the last fifty years, one is struck by the hostility evidenced by the "French colonies" to all administrators or residents who advocated a liberally directed development.

The underlying cause was the same in both instances, although the task accomplished by the French in a few decades in Morocco was incomparably superior to the one the protectorate had achieved in twice the time in Tunisia. The demands of the nationalists, of the Neo-Destour or of the Istiqlal, aimed at independence, and so at the exercise of authority by representatives of the Moslem population. Spokesmen for the French colonists deemed this transfer of sovereignty neither suitable to the interests of the people nor inevitable. As time went by, reforms became more difficult because the nationalist movement was growing and its demands bore upon the very thing that the French settlers were refusing: the restoration of complete sovereignty, either Tunisian or Moroccan. Neither in Tunisia nor Morocco did the French consent to become foreigners in countries they were conscious of having modernized. But by this refusal, which had no legal basis in the protectoral treaties, they ended by accelerating a change which could have taken place gradually.

For a long time the easy thing for the government in Paris was resistance. The ministers, in Paris, were or pretended to be haunted by the ghost of Munich or by the armistice of 1940. Immobilism, said some, resistance, said others; in any event, maintenance of the *status quo* by application of strong methods: General Juin off to Morocco, de Hautecloque to Tunis.

Two events brought on the break: the personal roles played by the Bey and the Sultan, and terrorism. The protectorate system assumed the consent of the sovereigns whose legitimacy France had recognized and whose thrones she had promised to protect when she proposed to modernize the states. From the moment when the sovereigns more or less clearly allied themselves with nationalism, nationalism had at hand a weapon whose dreadful effectiveness France was to experience. Beginning in December 1951 with the letter sent by the Quai d'Orsay to Chenik, then Tunisian Prime Minister and a member of the Neo-Destour, concerning the arrest of the Neo-Destourian ministers, the Bey opposed French plans, sometimes privately and sometimes openly, setting up a Grand Council of his own charged with the examination of the proposals of the Resident Governor, and making it known that when he granted his signature against his will he was yielding to constraint. Urban terrorism began in Tunisia after the failure of negotiations at the end of 1951, and French counterterrorism arose in reply. In 1954 a small number of Tunisians (between 2500 and 3000) took to the *maquis.*

In Morocco the same solidarity between the Sultan and the nationalist party was at the bottom of the crisis. General Juin had contemplated, as early as 1951, the possibilities of deposing the Sultan, utilizing the hostility of traditional circles toward a sovereign accused of bringing scandalous novelties into the life of the country. At the last moment he had to abandon this stratagem because of a veto from Paris. In the summer of 1954 a plot headed by a few highly placed functionaries of the Residency, in accord with the old Marrakech chieftain El Glaoui and certain Ulemas, managed the exile of Sultan Ben Youssef and his replacement by Sultan Ben Arafa. There followed two years of public disturbances, terrorism, and counterterrorism, and finally, after the return of the man who became King Mohammed V, Moroccan independence.

In the light of the outcome, now known, it is easy to insist that the best policy would have been to provide for the change, to admit that since Tunisian and Moroccan sovereignty had never ceased to exist, independence would be the final result of the French mission. Had this agreement been solemnly proclaimed, the nationalist parties would have been ready for compromise, at least in setting up a time program.

Such was the first version of the French overseas policy after the

Second World War. Taking the British policy of imperial withdrawal as a standard, we might explain the gap between the British norm and the French practice by circumstances—exaggerated nationalism, the haunting memory of surrender, the habit of direct administration, the opposition of the "colonies." This account of the matter does not seem untrue to me—personally, I am inclined toward such an interpretation—but I cannot forget that many Frenchmen, even after the event, do not accept the exemplary value of the British withdrawal or the inevitability of the final collapse.

*   *   *

Let us quickly pass on to the Franco-American debate, which comes out almost everywhere in the newspapers and in private conversations. As the French see it, the Americans are "colonialists" who have been successful: on the new continent they found a sparse population which finally wasted away on reservations, unable to adapt itself to the civilization of the invaders. The War of Independence against the United Kingdom having been the supreme American gesture, any revolt against a European power is compared with the national epic. Firmly allied with the Europeans of the Old World against the Soviet threat, the United States is in partnership with anti-European nationalism on other continents. When, having learned by experience, the Americans recognize that nationalism in Africa or Asia is neither democratic nor liberal, they plead the inevitable: it would be vain, in the modern world, to oppose the liberation of the colored races.

If we assume that they are right, the Americans should not be astonished that the French are not easily convinced. The doctrine which calls for giving up what one has conquered wins the approval of the onlooker more readily than that of the interested party. It is true that the latter is not so clear-headed, but the spectator too is often deluded by vast perspectives, forgetting that the will of those participating in the drama is a historical force. Has not the United States contributed to the creation of the fatality it invokes?

What perhaps seems most offensive in Paris is that American opinion confuses the moral with the pragmatic argument. Who can deny that the anti-European nationalists must win most of the time because they have the support of the Soviet Union, the Bandung coalition, and part of American public opinion, if not that of their leaders? But to succumb to propagandist slogans, to talk and act as though liberty were always incarnate in the nationalists and slavery in the Europeans, is to forget that, in states hastily organized and often without foundation, liberty and the security of the individual are sometimes even less respected than they were shortly before under foreign control. In many countries it is the Europeans who have brought with them the concept of the rights of man. Their withdrawal may bring with it the decline of European civilization and of the values it embodies.

The French, arguing *ad hominem* once more, observe that in East Africa, where British colonists have settled in Kenya and Rhodesia, there is no question of independence as in Ghana and Nigeria. Never, until recent years, had the European powers left important colonies at the mercy of governments which came from so-called indigenous populations.

Finally, the camouflaged domination Britain practiced in the Near East under the cover of theoretically independent yet unviable states, might indicate, if there were need to do so, that sovereignty is not enough to protect a people against foreign enslavement. But that kind of colonialism is more suitable for rich and powerful countries than for European powers who are weakened and poor. So the latter are tempted to believe that continued domination requires the maintenance of sovereignty. New states look elsewhere, away from their late masters, for inspiration, credits, and protection.

The debate between Americans and Europeans about their respective merits and misdeeds is ridiculous anyhow: the Americans were Europeans when they occupied a continent three-quarters empty. Let us leave to the historians the job of comparing the behavior of all these Europeans—English, French, and Dutch in North

America, Spanish and Portuguese in Latin America. Both groups imported slaves. Never, in past centuries, were American Indian populations treated as equals by the invaders, though the French and British did use them as allies in their warfare against each other when it was expedient to do so. The number of the conquerors compared with those of the original inhabitants determined the outcome, the resettlement of the natives in reservations or their enslavement within a society whose upper classes were of European origin. Americans and Europeans would be wrong to reproach each other for their imperialism or colonialism. The Americans of today are the descendants of Europeans neither better nor worse than those whose adventurous spirit attracted them to other lands.

The United States has not yet solved the problem inherited from the slave system of the past, the problem of integration into a Western society of millions of Negroes who want to become first class citizens. Even when, as in Brazil, the official doctrine is equality among individuals and race mixtures, the unwritten classification of people by color persists, with its train of humiliations and suffering, with inferiority the lot of some, and a more or less aggressive superiority the boast of others.

The Spanish destroyed the pre-Columbian societies to such an extent that revival was out of the question. The local representatives of the conquering peoples were strong enough to achieve their freedom from the tutelage of the mother country, and the Indian populations themselves had no prospect of advancing except in the newly independent Latin American states.

In Asia, the European conquerors had not found space three-quarters empty as in North America. They have not destroyed the old civilization or superimposed on the native peoples an immigrant upper class, which decided to settle in those distant lands. They have assumed the task of government and administration and exploited certain natural resources. Under this rule, sometimes brutal and sometimes paternal, the peoples of Asia took their first steps along the road to economic and technical modernization. The European empires in Asia could have lasted longer than they did—once established, an empire requires little to maintain. They were uprooted by the democratic ideals brought in by the conquerors themselves, fatally weakened by the wars in Europe. They were on that account no less the victims of accident, when viewed in the perspective of history.

Naval superiority made it possible for the Europeans to set up the first bases in the sixteenth century. European armies imposed their superiority in the eighteenth century. The anarchy which reigned in the Indian subcontinent and the decadence of the Mogul Empire facilitated the evolution of commercial establishments toward political domination. In the nineteenth century the Queen of England became Empress of India less as a result of studied determination or of a unified plan conceived and executed by the ruling class of the United Kingdom than because of favorable circumstances and the interplay of events. Moreover, the Europeans never committed great military forces to these distant ventures. The English in India, the Dutch in Indonesia, the French in Indochina needed only a small expeditionary corps which involved little expense compared with the troops they engaged in the "serious" wars on the Old Continent. Japan was admitted to the concert of great powers when she opened her doors to European trade and had undergone the historical mutations implicit in the adoption of Western civilization.

The diplomatic policy of the United States toward the Asian countries has differed from that of the European countries. This policy was the reflection of a new nation which viewed the relations of China, India, or Japan with Europe in the light of her own history and, above all, of her liberating revolution. Seen from Asia, however, the Americans often were no less imperialistic than the Europeans. Their missionaries strove to convert souls, their merchants to establish trading centers and make profits. Of course, Washington opposed the extreme forms of "Western imperialism," the seizure of sovereignty or the establishment of zones of influence. But as long as China did not have a government capable of developing her national resources and holding her own against foreigners, the motto of the "open door" and of respect for Chinese integrity often seemed like a technique, more subtle than, but not really different from, domination or exploitation. F. D. Roosevelt and his heirs urged the liquidation of the European empires in Asia after the Second World War, but Great Britain, given .the promises made during the war, would not have maintained herself by force while quelling the nationalist movement. Indian independence was to bring in its wake that of other countries of Southeast Asia.

Elsewhere the European conquerors created four kinds of situations: that in the Near East, where they began by freeing the Arab peoples from Turkish rule and carving out custom-made kingdoms for the Hashemite princes; the one in North Africa, where the French hesitated between administrative rule of the Asiatic type and the superimposition of a ruling class of European origin (South American type); third, the one in West Africa where only a small number of administrative officials, engineers, and government employees established themselves; and lastly, that in South Africa,[5] where a substantial white minority has been settled for centuries and has created a European society.

The British willingly represented themselves as anti-imperialists just after the first war, having cooperated with the Arabs against the Ottoman Empire. They granted independence to Iraq and Jordan and made the French mandates of Syria and Lebanon look "imperialistic." The contrast was glaring between the French attachment to direct rule and the British way of recognition of the sovereignty of states made susceptible to influence by the weakness or the personality of their rulers. A quarter-century later, nationalists denounce the British method as violently as the French administrative and military technique.

In Tunisia and Morocco the French had been too late in creating a situation which was neither Asiatic nor Latin American. In other words, they had not limited themselves to a form of administration

---

[5] The situations in Kenya and Rhodesia are somewhere between these last two.

which would be easily turned over to the nationalists who would some day be invested with sovereignty, nor had they destroyed the earlier civilization as was done in Mexico and Peru, but they had grafted a French society, including part of the Moslem mass and a small Westernized elite class onto Islamic society. The representatives of this French society have opposed both reform and the very inclination to come to an agreement with the nationalists, because such an agreement, whose object would be the restoration of Tunisian and Moroccan sovereignty, would inevitably destroy the privileges and even the status of French society established in an Islamic land.

The distant observer in London, Washington, or Paris pronounces the nationalist movement irresistible. Seen from Tunis or Rabat it did not appear so. Before the 1951 arrest of the Neo-Destour ministers in Tunisia and until the dethronement of the Sultan in Morocco, an army of a few tens of thousands of men seemed to guarantee the maintenance of order. Part of the Moslem middle class in both protectorates was cooperating with the French authorities. The settlers had no feeling that hostile populations, aroused against the oppressor, were impatiently demanding their freedom. Cartoons and propaganda to the contrary, reality is never simple. Habits and community interests are created in a few decades. Finally—and this argument is a strong one on a short-term basis at least—economic prospects were better for Tunisia or Morocco as part of a vast whole than for two independent countries lacking capital and technicians.

In Tunisia and Morocco, as we have said, the fundamental feature of the situation was the establishment of a French, Western-style society with a modern economy in a Moslem environment. A minority of Tunisians and Moroccans were integrated into the French society and, on the other hand, either directly or through a traditional bureaucracy, French officers or officials administered the Islamic community.

This state of affairs led to unending controversy in the realm of economics, with each side bringing forward equally irrefutable arguments. The chief arguments of those defending the protectorate were the importance of the task done by the protecting power, the part played by the investment of capital funds and by French experts and workers in modernizing the country, the superiority of results compared with achievement in independent Moslem countries, and lastly, the contribution of the French treasury to the administration and development of the protectorates.

Let us consider the case of Tunisia. There is no question that the presence of the French gave impetus to the economy of the country. The yearly average foreign trade in Tunisia before the protectorate was about 23 million francs; it rose to 54 million between 1881 and 1890, exceeded 73 million between 1891 and 1899. In animal husbandry, between 1881 and 1920 the figures rose, in thousands, from 166 to 537 for cattle, from 860 to 2,183 for sheep, and from 460 to 1,285 for goats. The number of olive trees grew from 7 to 12 million, olive production grew even faster, from between 6,000 and 8,000 tons to 35,000. Cereals covered 460,000 hectares in 1881 and more than a million when the protectorate ended, not counting 250,000 hectares cultivated directly by the French. Other products, negligible or non-existent in 1881, were later developed and now take the lead in the balance of trade: phosphates, iron ore, lead, zinc, salt, alfalfa, wine, preserves, canned foods. The official reports of the protectorate emphasized that Tunisia had, in proportion to its area and population, more roads, railroads, schools, doctors, and hospitals than Egypt, Iraq, or Iran. During the last years of the protectorate, the French treasury covered the Tunisian operational budget deficit (2 to 3 billion francs), and more than 10 billion francs were advanced by the Modernization and Equipment Fund for investment.

Morocco was transformed by the French protectorate, which lasted only about forty years. Moreover, this short period was interrupted by the two wars, and pacification was not achieved until nearly 1935. The infrastructure of carriageable roads (29,000 miles), railroads (1,100 miles), ports, and electric power plants was built mostly during the ten postwar years. During the period 1912–39, out of 270 billion francs' (1955 value) worth of public equipment, the French contribution was 200 billion, or about 75 per cent. The two postwar programs included about 150 billion francs in public expenditures for machinery, half of which was furnished by the Modernization and Equipment Fund. If to all this are added company capital investments, public loans to concessionary industrial and commercial companies, construction, and agricultural properties, the total invested capital comes to between 1,000 and 1,500 billion francs. During the last years of the protectorate, private and public investments in Morocco increased by 40 to 50 billion francs, of which the French treasury supplied nearly half. The deficits in the trade balance of the two protectorates—20 to 25 billion francs in Tunisia, and 40 to 50 billion in Morocco—give an idea of the size of the French contribution.

The nationalists did not deny this French help in the development of the country, but they reproached the French for having settled down as though in a conquered land, of having spent a great deal and built a great deal, but more for themselves than for the good of the Moslem populations. This reproach was partly unjust, for railways, roads, and electrical and industrial machinery remain in the states which have become independent; but it is true that the Tunisian and Moroccan masses had mostly remained outside the modernized sectors. In both protectorates the standard of living was low. In the French zone of Morocco the total personal income was estimated at 550 billion, or 65,000 francs[6] per capita per year. But this average figure means nothing, since in the modernized sector, the Europeans and Moroccans had incomes comparable to those in France, whereas living conditions tended to grow worse in the traditional sectors because of a rapid increase in the population (about 2 per cent a year).

If, before 1954, Morocco seemed to be in full process of expansion, it was not so in Tunisia. The period of the protectorate there divides into two phases, with the division coming about 1930. Until that time, the rise in population was moderate (9 per cent from 1911 to

[6] About $130 at current exchange rates. (L.E.)

1921, 14 per cent from 1921 to 1931), economic growth was comparatively rapid, and per-capita agricultural and mining resources increased. The relationship between population increase and economic
growth was reversed, beginning in 1930. In ten years, from 1936 to
1946, the population increased 25 per cent. Mine production was hit
by the world depression, then by the war. The lands on which an
additional effort could be made were kept infertile by an out-of-date
land system (*biens habous*). The farm methods of the native people
were hardly modernized at all. Looking at the nine chief products
(hard and soft wheat, barley, olive oil, wine, alfalfa, phosphate, iron,
lead) we find that between 1925–29 and 1948–52, the production
index increased 16 per cent, while the population rose by 56 per
cent. Resources per capita fell from an index of 100 to one of 74 in
twenty-five years.

Per-capita consumption did not decrease, however. Wheat consumption per capita went from 69 kilograms a year in 1926–30 to
86 in 1945–50. The same was true for olive oil, and imported products (sugar, per capita, 13.5 kilograms in 1947–51 as opposed to 12.7
in 1935–39; tea, 830 grams compared to 700; coffee, 880 compared
to 590; tobacco, 840 compared to 675). The inverse evolution of per-
capita output and consumption was made possible by French aid.

From this data, spokesmen for the protectorate and nationalists
again drew opposite conclusions. The former prophesied that the end
of the protectorate would aggravate economic difficulties—which has
in fact happened. Since the modern sector was essentially led and
financed by French personnel and capital, the departure of technicians and the cessation of capital investment by companies which
were now foreign would inevitably slow up or interrupt economic
development. To this the nationalists replied that they wanted freedom above everything, and that after the disturbances of the transi-
tory period they would be capable of managing their own country
without refusing foreign assistance.

In France, many observers of the Moslem world, without denying
the strength of nationalism, refused to see the wave of the future in

the independence of the protectorates. In an article in the review *Politique étrangère,* which we have used several times, the author quoted Mr. G. Hardy with approval: "True emancipation is not in the long run the spectacular and purely political gesture which would have us give up our authority. True emancipation, which we undertook to develop from the beginning, by giving social realities precedence over the formalism of institutions, aims at freeing the individual from paralyzing constraints and restores to him all his potentialities for development." And a little further on:

In the regrettable absence of an ideal more valid in our time, nationalism which responds to a longing for power by the elite and a need of equality in the masses, cannot be underestimated. Undoubtedly it may slow the investment of foreign capital indispensable for the betterment of the living conditions among local populations, just as it runs against the current of the general evolution of the world, which is characterized by the priority given to social and economic problems over political problems, and by the gradual grouping of peoples into unions of a federal nature. But within the country, nationalism is the support on which individual efforts will rely in the immediate future.

What conclusions did the writer draw from these seemingly contradictory statements? He declared that the problem was the same in the three North African countries and that it would be vain to distinguish "an Algerian policy of integration and a Tunisian or Moroccan policy of gradual emancipation." "If France weakens, the necessity disappears and revolt becomes a duty." France, then, must "guarantee her presence [there] by a show of strength which is to her advantage." "There is no ineluctable evolution of history," or at least the only ineluctable one is the one mentioned by a young Moroccan worker to a Frenchman: "The Moroccans of the *bled,* when you speak to them, answer you with respect because you are French: we, the young Moroccans, want no more of that respect."

Such was the state of mind of a Frenchman whom the conventional anti-colonialists called a colonialist. He was trying to defend the unity of the Franco-African bloc without failing to recognize nationalism, the aspiration for power by the elite and for equality by the masses.

Events decided against this effort to combine respect for nationalism with the maintenance of the protectorate. From the day when sentiment for equality became general, how was the protectorate to be justified? Believers called for freedom in the name of their revived religion; Moslems won over to Western ideals claimed it in the name of the "right of the peoples to self-determination." The French refusal was based on arguments of fact, not of principle.

Ineluctable evolution? It will never be proved, and at the time and in the way it came about, it was certainly not inevitable. But if nationalism is the springboard for individual efforts, might it lead to independence even if it does compromise economic growth and involve the risk of a lapse either into an orthodox Islamism tragically unadapted to the modern world or into a Russian or Chinese type of progress?

Such, a few years ago, were the uncertainties in which the experts on Islamic affairs were floundering, torn between a double conviction: of the strength of nationalism, and of the deplorable consequences, at least in Morocco, of giving up authority. Left to themselves, would the Moslem lands, deprived of technicians, be capable of continuing the struggle initiated and led by the French to develop politically, technically, and economically? Public opinion was as hesitant as the experts, parliamentarians were no surer than the experts, and the ministers reflected the parliamentarians' doubts. To maintain French authority and at the same time satisfy the demands of nationalism would have taken an inflexible determination to serve clearly defined goals. The result, unfortunate but forseeable, of so much subtlety in analysis and doubts as to what line of action to pursue, was an alternation between prolonged immobilism and impulsive activity. The nationalists, at least in Morocco, would gratefully have accepted the postponement of their triumph for a few years.

*   *   *

All the arguments that could be advanced against Tunisian and

Moroccan independence assume incomparably superior strength in the case of Algeria. The formula of the indissoluble bonds between the two communities, the land and the metropolis, applies there with increased force. The difficulty of negotiating with the nationalists is greater than elsewhere. The Algerian population is growing at the rate of 2.5 per cent a year. The soil can support two or three million people, and the population is nine million. Some 400,000 Algerians work in France; their wages support two or three million people across the Mediterranean.

The French citizens, numbering about 1.1 million, have a standard and style of living much like that of the French at home. They, too, like the French in Tunisia and Morocco, have built up a modern economy into which is integrated a minority (between one and two million Algerians), leaving on the outside the masses whose social organization is breaking down under the influence of Europe and of overpopulation. In the modern sector some 80 to 90 per cent of the capital funds and managerial personnel are French. Some twenty thousand Frenchmen own and cultivate 2,726,000 hectares; 630,000 Moslems cultivate 7,350,000. Of total public and private capital investment, estimated at 6,700 billion present-day francs, the Moslems' share would not exceed 10 per cent. One million Europeans pay as much in taxes as nine million Moslems. In short, modern Algeria is a French creation from which only a minority of the Moslem population has profited.

This is a truly diabolic situation, since the arguments of the two sides are in one sense equally valid. How could the French accept being foreigners in a land where they have lived sometimes for three generations? The very idea of an Algerian state governed by nationalists seems insane to them, since Algeria, they say, has never been a nation and nationalism is imported from the outside. But the wretchedness of the masses, in the eyes of the nationalists, carries with it the condemnation of France. Poor, illiterate, the Moslems of Algeria have had a feeble share in modern civilization, their customs have been shaken, the immemorial balance of resources and population has been forever upset, they have become acquainted with goods they did not have and could not help desiring. The privileged ones showed them the life to which they aspired and which is refused them. For long they have demanded individual equality between the members of the two communities. Today the equality to which the nationalists lay claim comes by way of the constitution of a state. It is in order that this state, which has no past, may have a future that the F.L.N. started the revolt.

The F.L.N. evolved from a section of the Movement for the Triumph of Democratic Liberties, commanded by the old Algerian chief Messali Hadj. It became, following four years of war, the principal politico-military movement in Algeria. In metropolitan France, among Algerian workers, the M.N.A., an organization recognizing the authority of Messali Hadj, still has partisans. The two rival parties both claim Algerian independence, the F.L.N. with more intransigence than the M.N.A. The F.L.N. also claims to be the only representative of the Algerian nation.

Spokesmen for the Algerian revolution declare that they were driven to violence by the failure of all attempts at reform. The statute of 1947 was not applied. The separation of the two electoral colleges, each electing the same number of deputies, belied the principle of individual equality, since it was the same as the proposition that one Frenchman equals eight Moslems. In addition, authorities deemed it necessary to "rectify" by their intervention the choice of Moslem voters. Measures which thirty, twenty, or even ten years ago would have appeased the dissatisfaction have become vain. From 1954 to 1958, as events developed, the French in Algeria officially subscribed to what they had obstinately refused: that is, the single electoral college, universal suffrage, the absolute equality of Moslems and French.

Algerian nationalism has no undisputed leader comparable to Habib Bourguiba in Tunisia or the Sultan of Morocco. The F.L.N. is a proletarian party, in its leadership as in its lower ranks, not a party under bourgeois leadership like the Neo-Destour and the

Istiqlal. It is more military, more radical, less inclined to compromise than were the other two nationalist parties of North Africa. The French government, after four years of armed conflict, cannot negotiate publicly with the F.L.N. as it did with the representatives of the Neo-Destour or of the Sultan.

Democratic procedures, with universal suffrage and the single electoral college, would inevitably lead in the long run to the election of a majority of Moslems, who would be more or less nationalistic. Whether these deputies sat at Paris or Algiers would change nothing: should they some day solemnly claim the right to constitute a State, even if it happened in the Palais-Bourbon, a French government, unless it was an authoritarian one, would have trouble resisting.

In 1956 57, none of the promises which at one time would have affected Algerian opinion had any influence on the course of events. The French offered individual equality at a time when self-determination—that is to say, equality between the communities—was in question. In 1958, the French in Algeria accepted the single electoral college, which they had always denounced as the preface to surrender, but they knew the F.L.N. to be opposed to any manner of "integration." What does the single college matter, since, unless there is complete victory over the rebels or negotiation with them, the war goes on?

*   *   *

In 1958, just before General de Gaulle's return to power, the French were in no better agreement on what they ought to do in Algeria and in Black Africa than they were on the causes of the tragedy of the Empire. Mendès-France, who was almost unanimously acclaimed when he signed the armistice at Geneva and solemnly granted Tunisia domestic autonomy, had become, as many Frenchmen saw it, responsible for our misfortunes. The speech at Carthage was in July 1954; two years later Tunisia and Morocco were independent and Algeria was on fire. The old sophism *post hoc, ergo propter hoc* offered itself to the bad faith of the truly guilty ones, those who had worn out the French army in a war it was impossible to win, those who had obstinately resisted the inevitable development in Tunisia, those who, in Morocco, had themselves, by dethroning the Sultan, given the nationalist party the support of the masses and precipitated the crisis from which the immediate independence of the country emerged.

In 1954, from January 1 to May 1, the losses of the French army and allied states in Indochina, in dead, wounded, and captured, were 38,130 men. During the following three months, until the cease-fire, the number of losses rose to 62,796. In less than seven months a hundred thousand men, probably about a third of the expeditionary force, had been put out of action. Reinforcements in 1952 amounted to 52,000 men, in 1953 to 66,000, in 1954 to 129,000.[7] Short of national mobilization, there was no way out in the summer of 1954 but the armistice. Even with mobilization France would not have been able to rebuild the Army in Indochina and reinforce the troops in North Africa simultaneously.

At the time of the Geneva armistice, the army in Tunisia numbered less than 20,000. Thanks to the armistice it numbered a little more than 44,000 by the end of the year. But even had the military potential been greater, circumstances narrowed choice to two alternatives: negotiation with the Neo-Destour Party, and acceptance of domestic autonomy, or resort to force, which would have delayed the end but would not have offered any plan for the future.[8]

When Edgar Faure negotiated in Morocco with Sultan Ben

[7] These figures were given by Jacques Chevallier, Minister of War in the Mendès-France cabinet.

[8] Jacques Chevallier recently published a report by General Blanc, Chief of the General Staff, dated 17 August 1954, from which the following is taken: "To try to suppress by force—even with reinforced units—a terrorism spreading progressively from the *bled* to the cities, without attacking its sources, local and foreign, that is, without solving the basic political problem, would have led France into another Bao-Dai experience, to a struggle without issue, as was the case in the Far East. The disastrous experiment carried out in Vietnam sufficiently proved, as had been predicted, the impossibility of mastering a popular movement by force without paying a considerable price. To adopt the same policy would have shaken the whole edifice in North Africa and endangered France's position in Europe."

Youssef and forced Ben Arafa to abdicate, insurrection was threatening in the hill country. Many who are today denouncing the surrender were then urging the leaders to negotiate so that the Algerian war would not spread to the Atlantic coast. The independence of Tunisia and Morocco gave the rebellion logistic bases, but the circumstances were such that, in 1955, withdrawal from the two protectorates seemed the only way of avoiding a general war in North Africa.

Historically, I consider the question settled. The immediate origin of the collapse of the French position in North Africa was the Indochinese war, the attrition of the army, the insufficiency of military means at the disposal of the authorities at a crucial moment. Taking a longer view, we see that the cause of the collapse, or at least of its suddenness, was the refusal of the French settlers to accept reforms whose final outcome would have been the independence of the protectorates. What might have come at the end of an evolution was granted at one blow.

Why was France incapable of foreseeing and organizing the transfer of the empire? Weakness of the regime, lack of authority on the part of ministers, resistance of popular opinion, national psychology? The choice of the sacrificial goat, the distribution of responsibilities among men, will always leave room for argument. The gravest result of retrospective polemics was to favor the worst interpretation: liberals and "Ultras" were equally inclined to believe that any negotiation would end in immediate independence, whereas immediate independence had been due to the incapacity of the Paris governments to negotiate in time. If, in Algeria, the alternative was to be independence or war, the war party won the day almost fatally, both because opinion rebelled at what seemed a national disaster and because the French in Algeria were powerful enough to forbid the leaders of the Fourth Republic to negotiate with the F.L.N.

Statesmen and experts had always insisted that North Africa was a unity. Tunisia and Morocco had been made subject to French law to guarantee the security of the borders of Algeria. Logically, the independence of Tunisia and Morocco should have prompted the French government to pursue a similarly inspired policy in Algeria. Psychologically, it was quite otherwise: they swore that Algeria would not meet the fate of the protectorates.

V ·❧

GRAVEDIGGER AND FOUNDER OF
TWO REPUBLICS

T HE chapter on French history from 1940 to 1958
could be entitled "From General de Gaulle to General de Gaulle"
or, if preferred, "From the Leader of Free France to the Dictator-
Legislator," who, under the auspices of the rebellion of the French
army in Algeria, received full power from the National Assembly
to write a new constitution.

Charles de Gaulle has buried two Republics, the Third and the
Fourth. The first time he did not succeed in imposing the sort of
constitution he considered necessary for the well-being of his country.
Because the Constitution of the Fourth Republic had not been made
by him, it was made *against* him. The Constitution of the Fifth
Republic, on the other hand, was made *by* and *for* him. So one may
well fear that these two constitutions embody opposite defects, the
first creating no counterweight against an Assembly all-powerful
yet often reduced to impotence by its dissensions, and the second
multiplying the precautions against those elected by direct universal
suffrage and entrusting to those elected by indirect suffrage—the
President of the Republic and the Senate—the responsibility of
decision and the power of veto.

Twelve years passed between the resignation of January 1946 and
the investiture of June 1958. Between those two dates General de
Gaulle took the lead in a "revisionist" party, the Rally of the French
People (R.P.F.), which he abandoned to its fate in 1953 in order to

retire to Colombey-les-Deux-Eglises. The resignation of 1946 was not good-bye to politics: the General expected that the deputies, unable to cope with events, would come to seek him out. When the 1946 Constitution had been ratified in spite of him, when circumstances were slow in making the appeal to the soldier inevitable, General de Gaulle tried to force matters. After some initially brilliant electoral successes, he failed. The hundred-and-thirty-odd deputies elected on the R.P.F. ticket were not enough to dictate their conditions. At the end of two years they had all been swallowed by the "system."

The crisis which General de Gaulle had always predicted but for which he had waited so long in vain was brought on by the Algerian war. The R.P.F. no longer existed, but there were still Gaullists in Paris and Algiers, and the General had again become a national hero, "the most illustrious of Frenchmen." In 1958 he gave France a constitution as he had passionately wanted to do for nearly twenty years, as he very likely would have been able to do twelve years sooner had he shown the tactical skill, moderation, and charm of which he has given so many proofs during recent months.

*   *   *

The revolution of May came at the intersection of two series of historical events, the aggravation of the political crisis caused by the absence of a majority in the National Assembly, and the prolongation of the war in Algeria. That the Fourth Republic would not withstand the loss of Algeria was readily admitted in the corridors of the Palais-Bourbon; it did not withstand the war, either. We prefer fascism to the independence of Algeria, said a few "Ultras"; for the time being, they succeeded in the liquidation of the Fourth Republic, but the man to whom they have given absolute power has the soul of a paternal monarch or of a prince-president, not of a tyrant.

The make-up of the Assembly, we have seen, reduced to less than four hundred the number of deputies capable of forming a government majority. Hence a majority had to include both the Socialist

Party and a large number of Independents. Ministerial crisis brought about a change of premier, and in part, of ministers, without any substantial modification of the majority itself. In normal times this situation would have been difficult; it became catastrophic when it was necessary to continue, win, or stop the fighting in Algeria. The cleverness, either unintended or diabolic, with which Edgar Faure got his Cabinet and the Assembly to absorb the shock of Moroccan independence, which neither one would have willingly tolerated, left a heritage of suspicion among the ministers and between the government and the Assembly. The Cabinet's freedom of action was further restricted. The "coup du Maroc" became an obsession. To suspect the ministers became a patriotic duty. The system was constantly threatened with paralysis.

The Socialist Party had campaigned in 1955 in favor of a negotiated settlement in Algeria, and had promised the demobilization of draftees. Guy Mollet named General Catroux, who was thought to be a liberal, as Minister Resident, and then went in person to Algiers. Welcomed by a near-riot, he yielded, accepted General Catroux's resignation, and put Lacoste in his place. Finally, after having first brought back a few tens of thousands of draftees, he undertook simultaneously a great military effort and secret negotiations with representatives of the F.L.N. The negotiations ran aground on the two chief issues: the F.L.N. demanded independence, or at least the right to it, and it insisted on being recognized as the representative, and the sole representative, of the Algerian people.

In the course of the years 1956 and 1957 the French army, some 400,000 strong, at once attempted to protect the population, to hunt down the armed bands, and to destroy the networks of the underground. It succeeded in overcoming urban terrorism, but not in eliminating the armed bands and the underground. In 1958, three and a half years after the rebellion had begun, the question was still whether it was possible to restore peace through total victory over the nationalists. How long would such pacification take, supposing it were possible? What political measures would promote it?

Neither popular nor parliamentary opinion was unanimous. Advocates of pacification were a little more numerous among the public than were those who wanted negotiation, to judge by the opinion samplings.[1] This was probably true in the Assembly as well, but minorities among the Socialists, the M.R.P., and the Radicals, and even secretly among the moderates, would have liked to see some kind of "political approach," a liberal status for Algeria which could attract the moderate nationalists. These half-liberals were denounced by the "Ultras," who, with the constant use of such terms as "abandon," "loss," "defeatism," spread a kind of political terror.

Now the "Ultras" held a triple veto. In the Chamber they had at least fifty votes available and were in a position to overthrow any government that would not bow to their will. Of course, the liberals could have returned the compliment, but the result would have been paralysis of the system in accord with the wishes of the "Ultras," who, from 1957 on, more or less consciously kept hoping for a constitutional crisis.

In addition to the veto in Parliament given them by the accidental make-up of the Assembly, there was the veto of the Frenchmen of Algeria. Provoked beyond measure by the guerrilla bands, the French in Algeria lived in dread, haunted by the thought of an Algerian "coup du Maroc." Once France had negotiated with the nationalists and the negotiation had ended with total independence for the two protectorates. This, in turn, had involved painful sacrifices for the French settlers and, in the end, their leaving. The French in Algeria believed that any negotiation at all with the nationalists was a step toward independence, and independence stood for total disaster.

Finally, in addition to the veto held by "Ultra" deputies and their allies, and the one held by the French of Algeria there was another decisive veto in case of need: the army's. This was the fundamental point. That the army might in certain circumstances refuse to obey and openly oppose a decision of the civil authorities had been suspected by many observers during the last two years of the Fourth

[1] In 1957. It is perhaps otherwise in 1959.

Republic; others refused to believe it. As for the parliamentarians, they were surprised by a revolution they had often prophesied.

Throughout the nineteenth century, the French army took part in the political vicissitudes of the country; it did not escape purges and counterpurges. But, considered as a social force, it took the initiative in no revolution, either in 1830, 1848, or 1870. Nor did it show any zeal in fighting for Charles X or for Louis-Philippe. Rulers were abandoned, in a few days or hours, by those who upheld their thrones—perhaps the rulers themselves gave up. The army never failed in an oath of allegiance which was not always directed to the same regime or the same person. The *coup d'état* of December 1851 is no exception: the President had trouble finding generals who would carry out his plan against the Assembly.

Under the Third Republic, the military, at the time of the Dreyfus affair and *"l'affaire des fiches"* [2] found itself involved in civil quarrels. Naval officers especially were considered to be mostly conservative or reactionary, perhaps even monarchist, in their opinions. But at no time was there a serious question of a military *coup d'état*.

From 1940 to 1944 the officers were put to an unprecedented test. After the defeat almost all of them chose to obey the legal government. They continued to obey in Syria and resisted the "aggression" by the British and Free French forces. The number of "dissidents" was larger in 1942, but obedience to legally constituted authority was nevertheless the password for most admirals, generals, and army and navy officers. Some important officers were severely and, as they saw it, unjustly, punished for having put nothing above discipline.

The Vichy government made the tragic error of not leaving the corps of officers out of politics and protected from ideology. De-

---

[2] The reactionary forces in the army and the country revealed by the Dreyfus affair produced a reaction of Republican defense. On his own responsibility, General André, who became War Minister in 1900, drew up *fiches,* or reports, on the Republican reliability of officers. The existence of the *fiches* and their use in the promotion of officers was revealed in 1904. The subsequent scandal led to the resignation of General André, and, indirectly, to the fall of the Combes government. (L.E.)

nunciation of the abolished regime, the Third Republic, propaganda against Great Britain, and the Pétain cult had made many converts to national revolution, especially in the navy. The soldiers could not have been reproached without injustice for a "politization" for which the ministers were responsible. Beginning in 1943 or 1944 the military were subject to propaganda of contrary import. The purge and the inactivation of key personnel were not of a nature to bring about the best sort of selection of officers. After 1945 the doctrine of passive obedience was no longer officially taught. If rebellion had been a duty in 1940, why should it not be one in 1958?

The bitterness of the officers is neither inexplicable nor inexcusable. For eight years they fought a thankless war in Indochina, without national support, thousands of miles from home. That war, in which so many of their number had fallen, ended in disaster, followed by a sordid settling of accounts between ministers and generals. The "system"—that is, the civil authorities, the press, and the parties accused of sympathy with the enemy—bore the responsibility, in their eyes, for so many vain sacrifices. In fact, certain military leaders had not realized in 1945-46 the nature of the adventure in which they were engaging the country any better than had the politicians. If they had all spoken the language of General Leclerc, if they had understood that to refuse war is sometimes the higher form of courage, if they had explained clearly in Paris what was possible and what was not, the collapse in the rice fields might have been avoided.

In Indochina a long campaign ended in humiliating defeat; in Tunisia and Morocco, skirmishes were followed by apparent capitulation. In neither of the two protectorates was agreement with the nationalists preceded by important military operations. In both places between 1952 and 1955, urban terrorism raged and was answered by counterterrorism. Fewer than three thousand Tunisian *fellagha* came to lay down their arms when the French government made that act the condition for continuing negotiations and when Bourguiba himself asked them to. In Morocco the partial dissidence of the tribes did not break out until August 20, 1955 and, a little later, the return of the Sultan brought with it the proclamation of independence. If independence is, for France, the same thing as "losing" the protectorates, then the "system" is responsible for having given up without fighting.

To the French army, Morocco had been the great achievement of the twentieth century. It was the army which had overcome tribal resistance, and which continued for the most part to govern. It was the army which inspired respect in the proud and warlike Moroccans. It was the army, not the civil administration, which had opened its ranks to young Moroccans (one of them was a general). It was in North Africa, and especially in Morocco, that officers had the feeling that they were carrying out a mission and occupying a place of honor. When, from one day to another, independence was granted to Morocco, the army obeyed, but with the feeling that the "system" was betraying the national interest.

In Algeria the army feels that it is fighting on the last line of resistance, the line which precedes irremediable decline. It has thrown itself wholeheartedly into pacification. It refuses to accept a defeat as at Dien Bien Phu, an inglorious retreat as at Suez, or a surrender without defeat as at Tunis or Rabat. Once again, this stand is easily understandable, and in itself, logical.

From the viewpoint of the military, any agreement with the nationalists would in all likelihood be even more odious than those in Morocco and Tunisia. The war there has been going on for four years and the means used by the *fellagha* are often horrible. Algeria is legally an integral part of the national territory; it is peopled by a million Frenchmen who have built up the country and who cannot conceive of staying there as foreigners. If Algeria, in its turn, becomes an independent state, then France will be reduced to the metropolitan hexagon, dedicated to a quasi-Spanish mediocrity. On the other hand, let Algeria remain under French sovereignty and everything again becomes possible: a confederation with Tunisia and Morocco, a way of access to the riches of the Sahara, a link with Black Africa. This time there can be no doubt: in Algeria national duty, dazzling in its clarity, must prevail over the rules of obedience.

The drift of the army toward political action also had other causes in the particular setting of the war in Algeria. Whether operations were called war or appeasement, they were essentially political as well as military. Setting aside the encounters with organized units of the Army of National Liberation, action against underground networks or terrorism is like that carried on in normal times by the police (checking identification papers, search, the pursuit of suspected malefactors, et cetera). If the officers are not content with this struggle against an elusive enemy, if they try to win the favor of the people, they must play the part of administrators and, even more, work out a design for the future. Who can be relied upon? How are community spokesmen to be chosen?

"Integration," in the current sense, means that the Algerian *départements* are to become more and more assimilated into France itself. The wretched conditions in the Algerian countryside impressed soldiers coming from France. The young officers were of socialist—not reactionary—inspiration and not prone to defend privilege or to shore up the defenses of the wealthy colonists. Since Algeria was French and was to remain so, since the nationalists who insisted on an Algerian fatherland were the enemy, the only way to reconcile the Algerians with their lot and to give a meaning and a pervading spirit to the process of pacification was to treat Algeria in actual fact like the other *départements* and Algerians like first-class citizens.

This war was political not only in its objectives and methods; it was so because of its geographic and diplomatic setting. In the same way that the North Koreans had profited by airfields shielded from bombardment in the "Manchurian sanctuary," and the Viet Minh divisions had been recruited, trained, and equipped in China, the F.L.N. had logistic bases in Tunisia and, to a lesser degree, in Morocco. What attitude was to be adopted toward the former protectorates? A friendly attitude was offensive to the officers, who were convinced that only Tunisian and Moroccan aid was preventing the wiping out of the rebels. A hostile attitude would have been contrary to the objective which the government continued to set itself:

namely, the maintenance of economic and cultural ties with Tunisia and Morocco. In Paris the ministers were sailing close to the wind, trying desperately to avoid the Charybdis of revolt by the army and the Scylla of a break with the former protectorates. In this dangerous navigation, Gaillard, and the Fourth Republic with him, ended by going to pieces on a reef. By their hesitation they angered everyone.

In Indochina, all French army elements had learned their lessons: Algerians and Moroccans had learned the methods of guerrilla warfare on the spot; officers, particularly those who had been prisoners of the Viet Minh, had personally experienced brainwashing and had learned the principles of subversive warfare (especially its two main aspects, psychological action and organization of parallel hierarchies). The similarity between the technique used by the Viet Minh and the F.L.N. finally convinced the officers that they again had the same enemy to contend with. It also gave them the desire to turn against that omnipresent enemy the very technique of subversion and organization the enemy had taught them.

Finally, added to all these joint influences were the activities of the politicians, who in person or through their agents spread truly revolutionary propaganda among the staff members and in the units of the army, denouncing the regime which was responsible for all the calamities and inciting the army to save the country. In May 1958, the army was far from united in a clearly determined plan, but it had in its ranks many conspirators who, abetted by representatives of the civil population, were awaiting a favorable time to assume power and confront metropolitan France with a *fait accompli*. The bulk of the officers who were not prepared to take the initiative of a *coup d'état* were ready to support the activists, and in any case resolved not to carry loyalty to the extreme of opposing their brethren who might have broken with the Republic.

After the fall of the Guy Mollet ministry France was living in a state of constant crisis. The two governments under Bourgès-Maunoury and Félix Gaillard were formed only after crises several weeks long and were the result of lassitude. It was necessary on the one hand to persuade Socialists and moderates to get along together, and on the other to satisfy the representatives of the various tendencies in regard to Algeria and Tunisia. Consistent with a custom which was not new, the graver the situation, the less chance group leaders had of attaining first rank. Because they aroused hostile feelings on one side or on the other, Pinay and Mollet were equally ineligible, and the Assembly had to fall back on second-rate individuals who would offend no one. The prestige of the executive was thus lowered by the choice of whoever became its temporary head.

The defection of the "Ultras" sufficed to put the government in the minority. So the Bourgès-Maunoury government was overthrown on account of the *loi-cadre,* and the Gaillard government in connection with the Anglo-American offer of mediation following the bombardment of the little Tunisian village of Sakiet. Bidault, summoned by the President of the Republic to form a cabinet, failed because he was an "Ultra," repudiated by his own party under the leadership of Pflimlin. Pleven failed when the Socialists refused to cooperate because of the assignment of the post of Minister of Defense to an "Ultra" opposed by other factions of the majority. When Pflimlin in his turn undertook to form a government, the situation appeared favorable to the conspirators. The premier-designate had the reputation of being a "liberal," and in his declaration of policy he called for negotiations at a favorable time in agreement with Tunisia and Morocco. On May 13 the oft-told happenings began: seizure of the government building, the organization of a Committee of Public Safety. For two days Fate seemed to hesitate. The generals in Algeria had not yet crossed the Rubicon. On the fifteenth of May General de Gaulle published his first communiqué, on the nineteenth Jacques Soustelle arrived in Algiers. From then on, the outcome was predictable and inevitable. The National Assembly invested General de Gaulle, legally, but under the threat of invasion by the paratroopers. Not a drop of blood had been shed. Was this a miracle accomplished by a wise people who had by now learned to carry out revolutions without violence, or the inglorious ending of a regime which found no defenders? Probably both at the same time.

*   *   *

The May revolution may be considered from three points of view because it has a triple meaning. With respect to Algeria, it is the only case of a revolution forced on the mother country by a minority of colonists, as though the Irish Protestants of Ulster had tried to overthrow the Westminster Parliament, which had consented to negotiate with the Irish nationalists. For the Fourth Republic it was the end of a short and disturbed existence. From the standpoint of history, it proves that in the twentieth century, as in the nineteenth, France has not found a form of government which obtained general support.

The direct cause of the revolution was not so much the weakness of the Fourth Republic as it was the tragedy of Algeria. It is not certain that even a more solid republic could have coped with it. The expense of the war in Algeria does not exceed the resources of the country. From a gross national product, at market value, of 20,520 billion francs (1957), France can, if she so decides, spend seven or eight hundred billion francs in Algeria, half of which comes as a deduction from military spending in France herself and in Germany. The major difficulty is political and psychological. Democracies have never upheld all freedoms in time of war. Beginning in 1956, young Frenchmen were doing their military service in Algeria. Yet part of the press continued to denounce the methods of repression and even pacification itself. Sooner or later the contradiction between war and democracy had to be resolved.

At the Palais-Bourbon and in Algiers, ministers and deputies, passionately eager to keep Algeria French, and also imbued with ambition, relied on exploiting the anxiety of the French people and bitterness in the army as a means of extortion against their opponents, and as a weapon against the regime. Lacoste, the Governor

Resident, declared that he alone was capable of stopping the revolt
of the French in Algeria, which he was at times encouraging in
private. The greater the threat became, the more indispensable and
irremovable he himself became.

The French in Algeria, alone, amounted to nothing. Algeria,
especially Algeria at war, cannot survive a week without supplies
from the mainland. But from the moment the army had a feeling of
solidarity with those million Frenchmen settled in an Islamic land,
colonists and soldiers together constituted an almost irresistible
"pressure group." The aim of the Paris government was the defeat
of Algerian nationalism: now it would have immediately lost the
war it wanted so desperately to win had it gone into direct conflict
with the army command. When, on the morning of the fourteenth,
the ministers suggested a blockade of Algeria, generals and admirals
in France quietly but stubbornly refused.

There has been and will continue to be much discussion about who
was responsible. The helplessness of the public authorities in Algeria
preceded the thirteenth of May; it was tolerated, if not consciously
desired, by Governor Lacoste. In part this helplessness resulted from
the war itself: the paratroopers had won the battle of Algiers by
ruthless methods and by taking upon themselves the functions of
the police. The arming of the French population gave the most
extreme partisans of the colonists a means of coercion and shock. In
Paris the ministers had justified operations they did not approve
(Sakiet) and which exceeded the directives (after the event some
generals had expressed regret for having obeyed orders from Paris
during the Suez expedition). The power of decision had slipped
away from the government and now lay with the military leaders,
and not always with those of highest rank among them. Everything
conspired to undermine the prestige and authority of the government
of the Republic: the selection of men, the absence of a majority, the
internal contradictions of the Cabinet.

If one asks whether the Fourth Republic succumbed to its own
vices or to an accident, the answer is inevitably lacking in polemical

simplicity. The regime was weak because there was no coherent majority in the Assembly, where the power lay. But can a government based on popular opinion be strong when the citizens are not agreed on fundamentals? The Constitution ought to have made some provision against the dispersion of parties and opinions. It did not do so. Two questions, however, still persist: is a democracy capable of waging a war of which an important element in the country disapproves? Even with a strong government, can the war in Algeria be won?

Whatever consideration is given to the origin of the events of May, to the "return of the colonists" and to the structural defects of the regime, the fact remains that the Republic which was restored in 1944 had not retained the legitimacy of consent which it seemed to have gained after the First World War. The loss of the empire having assumed the character of a national disaster for part of the people, forces similar to those which had brought Marshal Pétain and his crew of traditionalists to power in 1940 came into play in favor of General de Gaulle. By an irony of history he begins a second career in circumstances which in certain ways resemble those of 1940. But the Marshal could not save France by negotiating with the Germans, whereas the General can save France by ending the war in Algeria.

In 1940 the brutality of military defeat had left all France dumbfounded. The political leaders who advocated continuation of the war overseas had given way to the advocates of an armistice, and the latter had chosen Marshal Pétain as their symbol, if not as their guide. With that strange fickleness of public opinion characteristic of France, the Republic, political parties, and parliamentarians seemed to have disappeared into thin air. The responsibility for the catastrophe fell back on the form of government and not on the military leaders and, reading the newspapers and sometimes even listening to conversations, one might think that the generals were innocent and the deputies alone were to blame. As for Marshal Pétain, he profited by the prestige of age and of past services. The mass of Frenchmen unloaded onto him the cares of public affairs. Some counted on him to collaborate with the Germans, others to resist them.

The ambiguity is even more profound today. A few months ago, the liberals were hoping for General de Gaulle's return to power because they thought he had been won over to their way of thinking. Remarks he had made in private were quoted (" . . . they deserve independence because of the way they fight for it"); his interview with the Tunisian ambassador and his friendship with people in all camps were remarked upon. People read Bourguiba's appeal to the only man who could get the French to negotiate with the nationalists without humiliation. But at his first press conference the General spoke of Robert Lacoste, his friend. Was the support of Michel Debré, of Georges Bidault, of Jacques Soustelle the result of misunderstanding? General de Gaulle, like Marshal Pétain not long before, could represent everybody only by wrapping himself in the mystery of consciously enigmatic language. Before the event he had, by the way he talked, given hope to all factions. During the first weeks of his reign he did his best, not unsuccessfully, to keep alive the doubts of some and the hopes of others.

Again like Marshal Pétain, General de Gaulle is supported at the start by two teams or two schools, if we set aside the widespread, almost unanimous consent of the majority: moderates and "Ultras," traditionalists and revolutionists, those who were known as the men of Vichy and the men of Paris. The colonels and the committees of public safety in Algiers now take the place occupied nineteen years ago in Paris by those who were calling for a truly socialist revolution in contrast to the conservative national revolution. As in 1940, the governmental personnel in 1958 unites survivors of the "system" (in 1940 the expression was the "abolished regime"), the leader's intimates, reformers made bitter by long waiting, and, finally, a few important civil servants.

The comparison will seem insulting only to those who forget the Marshal's popularity in 1940, and the discredit into which the parliamentary regime had fallen. The revolutions of the nineteenth century, the change from one monarchy to another or from monarchy to republic, had always seemed mysterious to me in spite of the history books. Why did a Parisian riot make a king take flight? Why did a few shots along the boulevards cause a throne to fall? I could not understand the want of proportion between the initial incident and the outcome. The events of May 1958 showed me the connection.

The regime is so undermined by the criticism of its adversaries and the indifference of its supporters that it is at the mercy of any shock. Two days of rioting, and King Louis-Philippe found himself alone. Mob scenes in Algiers, endorsed by the military authorities, were enough to make the government in Paris, unquestionably legal, with all powers at its disposal in theory, feel that it had no support. The mass of the country was entirely calm (so it was at the time of the Revolutions of 1830 and 1848), but the servants of the State stopped obeying the orders of the government. Neither the army nor the civil service revolted in May 1958. Either actively or passively, generals and admirals kept the ministers from imposing their wills upon the committees of public safety in Algiers.

The similarity between the situations in June 1940 and May 1958 is only partial. In both cases, an atmosphere of national catastrophe; in both cases, discredit of the parliamentary system held responsible for all misfortunes; both times those who offer themselves as saviors could as well be considered gravediggers (were the army chiefs entirely blameless in 1940? Did not the spokesmen for the French in Algeria, who had opposed all the reforms proposed by the mother country in fifty years, provoke the rebels, with whom they today insist it is impossible to negotiate?). Both times, right-wing traditionalists and revolutionaries came to power favored by circumstances because the laboring masses who follow the Communist line were excluded from the community, and the republican parties were disqualified by events. In the void thus created, little groups of fascists, politicians who have revolted against parliamentary impotence, become, for a time, historic forces.

Similarities end at this point. To begin with, there is a difference of personality on which it is scarcely worth insisting. Marshal Pétain, more than eighty years old, could not really be a leader. In all governments by personal power, associates play a considerable role. When the leader himself is too old to dominate men or events, everything depends or seems to depend on his advisers. The rivalry to get into the "inner circle" creates no less uncertainty than does the parliamentary struggle. The contrast between the authority the old man claims to exercise over others and his weakness toward his intimates and himself sharpens. General de Gaulle, by May 1958, had lost something of his severity but nothing of his ascendancy over men, nothing of his will power, of his power to command and to convince. In 1958, as in 1940, some of the politicians desired and most of the country was ready to accept a dictator (in the Roman sense) who for a limited time would make unaided the decisions which would bind the whole community. Marshal Pétain was the symbol rather than the incarnation of the dictator. General de Gaulle is, and wants to be, the dictator who, in conformity with law, exercises absolute power and reforms the institutions of the Republic.

In 1940 the disaster was real and the country was occupied by the enemy. In 1958 the disaster is mostly psychological. It is for Frenchmen themselves to fix the direction events will take. The independence of Tunisia and Morocco is not in itself a catastrophe. If mutual understanding with the nationalists of these Islamic lands was inevitable and is still possible, the end of the protectorates, whatever sacrifices may be involved for the French colonists, is only an episode; it ends an era; it does not mean the end of French "presence."

Marshal Pétain let some people understand that his heart was with the collaborators, others that his best wishes were for the Gaullists. He maintained this ambiguity until November 1942; it was not yet entirely dissipated in August 1944. The role assigned to him by history does not allow a clear definition of what he meant, even for posterity.

Of course, actions cannot be neutral or ambivalent to the same extent. Marshal Pétain's course involved some collaboration with the

Germans, but it was partially imposed by the events: since the French government had stayed on French soil, it had to give pledges to the enemy. Did these pledges go beyond what was inevitable? No one knew with certainty. General de Gaulle was imposed by the Algerian rebellion on an Assembly which invested him legally but under a threat. Those who brought him to power have loudly declared themselves advocates of "integration." The expression, a revival of the old password "assimilation," had become popular with the French in Algeria to the extent that it designated the exact opposite of independence. Of the two forms of equality—individual and collective—the first was all the more acceptable since means were not lacking to use it as a ruse.

The ambiguity lies not only in General de Gaulle's intentions toward Algeria; it is in the very meaning of his undertaking. What, in 1958, is the equivalent of the resistance of 1940? To struggle to the bitter end against Algerian nationalism while coming to terms in the rest of the world with Arab or African nationalism? Or to seek a compromise with people who crave a country of their own? Is resistance embodied at home in the supporters of the military, who are opposed to parliamentary methods, or in the republicans who denounce the rebellion of the military leaders? On which side does General de Gaulle himself stand? On neither side, the faithful followers answer. General de Gaulle stands above it all because he is France herself. Such is, effectively, the mythology accepted by popular opinion. When France is weary of her partisan jousting she comes back to her old dream of a power above parties, a Caesar for lack of a king. But General de Gaulle is, by rational conviction, committed to the Republic. The Gaullist Republic, to be sure, has little in common with the "system," or even with the Republic of the republicans.

*   *   *

The Constitution approved on September 28, 1958, has been characterized by its authors as establishing a parliamentary regime based on the separation of powers. Certain commentators have defined it as a compromise between presidential and parliamentary government. Both definitions contain some truth; both miss the point.

It is true that every effort was made to separate the powers, both as to their sources and to their functions. Only the Assembly is elected by direct universal suffrage; the President and Senate are elected in two steps, according to a procedure which favors the rural districts over the cities. As for the Constitutional Council, it is named by the Presidents of the Republic, of the Senate, and of the Chamber of Deputies; it is not elected. To keep the National Assembly from again assuming total power, the Constitution lists the only matters which are subject to legislative action and allows the government to appeal to the Constitutional Council against any eventual attempts by a future Assembly to go beyond the limits imposed on it.

On paper, the President of the Fifth Republic will not be the chief executive, as is the President of the United States. But the comparison is unimportant. In practice, the election of the President in the United States takes place by universal suffrage, incidental to nomination by the parties. Thus, the American president may claim a popular mandate; he is the leader of one of the two great parties. The danger of conflict between the executive and the legislature is thus reduced. This is not the case under the French Constitution.

In order to understand the Constitution of the Fifth Republic it is best, I believe, to refer to the intentions of those who framed it, to the interpretation they made of the crisis in France, and to the objectives they had in mind. General de Gaulle himself, in spite of what may have been said, has never wanted a presidential government; he has never explicitly formulated the concept of responsibility of the ministers to the President of the Republic. He has always considered a Chief of State as one who would not be reduced to the mere performance of ceremonial functions or doomed to the daily management of public affairs. The Chief of State, according to the desire and practice of General de Gaulle, is a sort of king who intervenes in grave emergencies and makes major decisions, but leaves the thankless task of managing the economy and getting the consent of the National Assembly to a Prime Minister whom he has himself chosen.

The text of the Constitution is in full accord with the wishes of General de Gaulle on this point; the President of the Republic will be comparable to a king in the constitutional monarchies of a century ago or the prince-president of a Bonapartist republic. Elected for seven years, he is to be responsible to no one but history, unless he is impeached before the High Court for treason. He chooses the Prime Minister; he alone can dissolve the National Assembly and submit laws passed by the Parliament to a referendum; he disposes personally of the right to pardon; he negotiates and ratifies treaties, and he is, it seems, given the power to conclude military agreements which do not require parliamentary ratification. In exceptional circumstances he assumes all powers and puts himself by his own decision into the position of dictator, in the Roman sense. More than an arbiter and less than an American-style chief executive, he may, depending on the circumstances, the moment, and the personalities involved, impose himself as a monarch or gradually become like the president of the Third Republic.

The Constitution has another progenitor, Michel Debré, supported by survivors of the "system," the Ministers of State, Guy Mollet, Pierre Pflimlin, Louis Jacquinot, and Félix Houphouët-Boigny. Debré himself, according to previous statements, would have liked to go all the way with the presidential concept, and make the ministers responsible not to the National Assembly but to the Chief of State. This provision was barred by the very terms of the law granting constituent authority to the government presided over by General de Gaulle. So it was that the framers multiplied the precautionary measures against the Assembly and ministerial instability.

Certain provisions, often demanded by reformers, tend to correct parliamentary practices. In this first category belong the personal ballot, the limitation of sessions, which are restricted to five and a half months a year, and, finally, the injunction against deputies or senators who are named as ministers keeping their seats. If ministerial instability was due, among other things, to the "rush for portfolios," this rule should help cut down the incidence of crises.

Other provisions have in view an improvement in the relation between executive and legislature. It was often complained that the Assembly spent months debating the budget. From now on the Assembly will have seventy days in which to vote it. If it has not reached agreement in that length of time, the administration promulgates the budget by *ordonnance*. There was complaint that the legislature went into administrative detail and voted into law measures which in fact should have been adopted by decrees or *règlements*. The Constitution specifies what matters shall be subject to legislation and leaves to the government the last word on questions which the Constitutional Council will deem statutory, *règlementaires*. Other provisions strengthen the authority of the government over the Parliament: although the province of the law is strictly limited, the government may also receive a legislative delegation; it may oblige Parliament to decide by a single vote on all or a part of a text under discussion; it may engage the responsibility of the ministry on a proposal which, in such a case, is automatically adopted unless a motion of censure gets an absolute majority of votes in the Assembly (thus a law may be adopted although it has not received a parliamentary majority).

Finally, since the principle of ministerial responsibility has been maintained, other provisions have been made to prevent instability, which is considered the fundamental evil. The life of the government can be challenged only by a motion of censure signed by at least a tenth of the members of the Assembly. This motion is considered passed only on condition of having won an absolute majority of votes, the majority being calculated on the total number of deputies and not on the number voting. In other words, a government receiving a minority vote still remains in office unless its opponents have won 251 votes in an Assembly of 500 deputies. Finally, if a vote of censure has failed, those moving it can make no other such motion during the same session.

Such, then, are the three series of principal provisions by which the constituents hope to reform Parliament, to strengthen the executive in relation to the legislature, to prevent guerrilla warfare by deputies against the ministers, and give governments stability and authority.

On paper, this Constitution is open to many objections. While appealing to the principles of democracy and universal suffrage, it plays hocus-pocus with the source of its legitimacy by weakening those elected by direct suffrage, and strengthening the beneficiaries of indirect suffrage. The Senate, which because of the way it is chosen has always been more conservative than the Chamber of Deputies, recovers four of the powers that it had under the Constitution of 1875 and which the Constitution of 1946 had curtailed. In case of disagreement between Senate and National Assembly, the latter prevails only if the government decides in its favor. The government, by falling back on the Senate, can block indefinitely any reform called for by the Chamber. The Fifth Republic is more conservative than that of 1875.

This constitution differs fundamentally from those of all Western countries. In Great Britain as in the United States, in Germany as in Sweden, the chief executive receives, through the parties, a popular mandate. Since legitimacy is democratic, direct universal suffrage gives governments their authority. There is nothing of the sort in the Fifth Republic. Neither the President of the Republic, nor the Prime Minister, nor the Constitutional Council, has received directly any popular mandate. Only the Assembly has been elected by the citizens, and it is the prisoner of a web of obligations and prohibitions.

I am well aware of the difficulties the writers of the Constitution faced. In order to function, democracy, whether it be parliamentary or presidential, requires that the party system manifest a common will. Laws alone do not lead citizens and political leaders to organize a few large parties capable of concerted action. The authors of the Constitution began with the assumption that the Assembly would be hopelessly divided, at least during the first days of the Fifth Republic, but that it would perhaps accept what it would not have been capable of deciding itself. The separation of powers, as it was set up, goes against the current of historical development in the West. Even in the United States, where it inspired the founding fathers, it has been balanced by the two-party system. In France it appeared as a needed expedient until the moment when an election law requiring an absolute majority would gradually have simplified the political picture and brought from the ballot boxes a majority, a program, and an expressed will.

On paper, this Constitution threatens to provoke conflicts of three sorts: between the President and the Prime Minister, between both of them together on one side and the Chamber of Deputies on the other, and between the opinions of electors and the actions of those elected—since the deputies who are chosen by direct suffrage are rendered helpless by those elected by the indirect vote. The future of the regime will be determined essentially by the relations which are established between the President and the Prime Minister. If the President prevails, the regime will develop in the presidential direction, and the Assemblies will have to be satisfied with a secondary role. If the Prime Minister gains the ascendancy, the government will tend to become parliamentary, and the Assemblies will not resign themselves to the diminished standing the writers of the Constitution have imposed on them. Yesterday, revisionism came from the right; tomorrow it will come from the left.

In theory, the Constitution complicates rather than simplifies General de Gaulle's task. With no matter which Constitution—that of the Second, Third, or Fourth Republic—the General could have governed France for a few years, either as President of the Republic or Premier. Only the Constitution of the Fifth Republic divides the executive power between two men. For the time being, the Chief of State, not the head of the government, will be the real leader.

Had he yielded to the solicitations of some politicians and consented to remain at the Hotel Matignon[3] for a few years while René Coty prolonged his sojourn at the Elysée, General de Gaulle himself would have repudiated his efforts. The keystone of the Gaullist Republic is, and can be, only the President of the Republic. Doubt is all the less permissible because the President of the French Republic is, at the same time, the President of the Community and the Community, on paper, will be ruled by a presidential constitution. The ministers of the Community will not be responsible to the Senate; they will be the spokesmen and executive agents of the President. The responsibility of the Cabinet to the French Chamber of Deputies is, in the present Constitution, an added feature. It does not follow that in the long run this responsibility will not be a decisive factor in constitutional procedure.

*   *   *

Between the beginning of June 1958 and early January 1959, General de Gaulle had practically absolute power as Premier: parties and Parliament no longer existed, a vast majority of the public had confidence in him, the Assemblies were adjourned, and no one could oppose him. Only the world—things, if you wish—had not changed and continued to provide obstacles.

France had delegated to General de Gaulle the mission of finding a cure for a crippled regime, an ungovernable legislature, and some seemingly insoluble problems. The former Free French leader was resolved to draw up a constitution because for years that had been his ambition and because our history offered innumerable precedents since 1789. But new institutions were only a means.

In the African territories south of the Sahara, new institutions were seen to offer a chance to reconcile the maintenance of the empire with the spirit of the times. In 1956, at the very moment when he was hurling all France into the attempt to pacify Algeria, the government of Guy Mollet enacted the *loi-cadre*. According to law, each of the

---

[3] Headquarters of the Premier. (L.E.)

territories grouped into the two federations of West and Equatorial
Africa was granted a sort of domestic autonomy (an elected assembly
and government, in fact responsible to the Assembly, were gradually
substituted for colonial administration). Two years later the movement for emancipation had become stronger and the African parties,
all in favor of maintaining close relations with France, were heatedly
discussing two subjects, two terms fraught with feeling: independence and regrouping (or primary federation). Had the moment
already come to go through the succeeding stage which would lead
from autonomy to independence? Would each of the territories
(Senegal, the Ivory Coast, and so on) be independent or would
primary federations each include several territories, with these federations together forming federal or confederative ties with France?

Political circles even in France hesitated between the two conceptions. According to one school of thought the development from
autonomy to independence was inevitable: it would be better to give
immediate and voluntary assent to the principle of independence
and negotiate with the African delegates about the methods of
federation and confederation. According to another school, an independent territory was "lost" when the tricolor was lowered and the
French army withdrew. Now only the Westernized intellectuals,
expressing not authentic grievances but resentful animosity and
demagogy, demanded an inevitably fictitious sovereignty to which
the masses themselves would be indifferent. The first school wanted
to negotiate the constitution of the French–Black African Community with the representatives of the principal parties (*Rassemblement
Démocratique Africain, Parti du Regroupement Africain*), the principle of independence having been agreed on. The second school
would have granted a gradually increasing autonomy without raising
the issue of French sovereignty.

General de Gaulle chose an intermediate solution. In his initial
plan he was close to the arguments of the second school of thought.
The plan, in effect, granted the territories in Africa a so-called
federal status which in its essentials upheld the domestic autonomy

of the territories and French sovereignty in military and diplomatic affairs and, in part, in economic matters. Under pressure from African delegates in Paris and from crowds during his trip, de Gaulle was led to recognize the inalienable right to independence of all territories in Black Africa. By voting *non* to the constitutional referendum of September 28, a territory chose secession and automatically became independent. By voting *oui,* it declared its will to remain within the French Union and reserved the choice between the status of a *département,* internal autonomy, and the status of a free state, belonging to the Community. The positive answer did not forfeit the right to independence. At any time, any member state can leave the Community if the territorial assembly so decides by a majority vote and if the people approve in a referendum.

All the territories voted *oui* by impressive majorities except Guinea, which voted *non* almost unanimously, following the appeal of Sékou Touré, a labor leader expert in the techniques of mass organization, who has traveled behind the Iron Curtain. Now, Guinea's *non* cannot fail to resound throughout French Africa.

General de Gaulle had emphatically pointed out the antithesis between the meanings of *oui* and *non.* The territories which stayed in the Community would continue to receive French administrative and financial aid; those refusing adherence would accept the risks of secession—in other words, they would be left to their own resources. Outside of the Community the Constitution provided that independent states which wanted to maintain relations with France could enter an association whose terms were, however, not made specific. Sékou Touré, after September 28, immediately proposed association to the government in Paris. The latter put off a decision; either acceptance or refusal offered all-too-evident risks.

Of all the territories in Black Africa, Guinea held the most trump cards, because of its enormous deposit of bauxite, the exploitation of which had already begun. If France decided to break all ties with Guinea and requested businessmen to halt their investments and technicians to withdraw, the tens of billions already spent would be lost unless—and this was more probable—foreign capitalists or the Soviets should come to fill the vacuum. Viewed from another angle, if an agreement for an association carried with it advantages comparable to those of the Community, the other territories would not resist the temptation to follow Sékou Touré's example. His success seemed hardly less dangerous than his failure. In one case, he would set an example, in the other he would make every effort, with Soviet aid, to bring about the break-up of the Community.

The French government cannot fail to discriminate between those who join the Community and those who secede. But it would be a mistake, it seems to me, to stake everything on those political leaders of Black Africa who, having chosen the Community, see in the independence of Guinea a dangerous precedent and in Sékou Touré an enemy. Whatever the inconveniences of compromise, they are less than those of a total break. In the long run the goal must be to overcome, not widen, the split between states that are members of the Community and the associated states.

If the example of Guinea were unique, one could, if necessary, maintain the strict alternative: the Community or secession. But Togoland and the Cameroons are to attain independence in 1960, at the same time as British Nigeria. Madagascar will enjoy a special status close to independence within the Community. The objective is not to set up obstacles to independence, but to organize the change so as to avoid chaos, and safeguard the chances of a Franco-African Community, whatever its legal expression.

French public opinion, in spite of the activities of a few troublemakers, has scarcely reacted either to the right of secession solemnly granted to Black Africa or to the secession of Guinea. Attachment to colonial possession, passionate refusal to surrender, the conviction that loss of empire means decadence—all these feelings seem to have been expressed and exhausted with respect to Algeria. The main reason for this difference in attitude seems to me to be less the oil wealth of the Sahara or the strategic importance of Algeria than the presence of a million Frenchmen north of the Sahara, and the war itself. The loss of Algeria would arouse less bitterness than the loss of the war. Once the war was won, many officers would probably accept a so-called liberal solution. But for nothing in the world would they yield to the F.L.N.

The conciliation of imperial desire with concessions to the spirit of the times was relatively easy in the case of Black Africa, because it had been prepared by the Fourth Republic and one could easily satisfy African aspirations without shocking domestic opinion. The French in Algeria and the army had overthown the Fourth Republic because they thought it unable to wage the war, because they suspected it of harboring the thought of surrender. How could General de Gaulle have put an end to the war in a few months if, in the short run, an agreement with the F.L.N. was the only way to restore peace?

For a few hours the miracle of a peace acceptable both to the F.L.N. and the French citizens and officers in Algeria seemed about to be achieved. The triumphant referendum of the twenty-eighth of September had given General de Gaulle unrivaled authority, and had weakened the F.L.N. locally and in world opinion. The publication of the letter to General Salan had apparently confirmed the abolishment of the committees of public safety, the restoration of civil authority and the end of political action by the army. When, at his press conference, General de Gaulle called for the peace of the brave and invited Ferhat Abbas to Paris, enthusiasm won over the press of the whole world, not just the French press. For twenty-four hours the Chief of State was applauded by the whole Western world. He could have remained at this victorious peak of glory only by a glorious peace in Algeria. When the "Algerian Government" in exile refused the invitation, when the failure of the magic operation became apparent, General de Gaulle fell back to earth. Like those who had gone before him, he could not overcome the dilemma: either he had to negotiate with the F.L.N. (but to do so he would have to broach the possibility of a national Algeria) or he would not negotiate with the F.L.N. (but then how long would it be necessary to carry on the war?).

Did an intermediate solution almost appear? Had the F.L.N.

promised to respond to General de Gaulle's invitation to come to
Paris to negotiate a cease-fire? Did President Nasser and the Soviets
urge the F.L.N. not to consent to a meeting? (I do not believe
there was any such pressure.) Did the agents who had carried on
the semiofficial bargaining entertain illusions about the thoughts or
reservations of one side or the other? Did they create the misunderstanding? Or did the unfortunate phrases ("white flag," "safe conduct") aired by the newspapers in Algiers prompt intransigence on
the part of the F.L.N. leaders who had been willing to compromise?
It is difficult to answer with certainty (even when one has known
part of the secret negotiations).

The dispute over form symbolizes the disagreement as to substance. One of the two things is true: either General de Gaulle was
discussing with the F.L.N. leaders only the terms of a cease-fire,
and in that case his offer was an exact duplicate of the one Guy
Mollet had made, and amounted to a demand for political capitulation. If our adversaries laid down their arms without the fate of
Algeria having been decided they would be throwing themselves on
our mercy. Or else, the President of the French Government was
discussing the future status of Algeria with the envoys of the "government" in exile, and in that case even if the word "independence"
was not used, the F.L.N. was given a kind of "representativeness,"
and Algeria a sort of national standing. One does not negotiate with
rebels except on the terms of their surrender. If one negotiates with
them one no longer looks upon them as rebels; implicitly one
recognizes them as future ministers of an autonomous, if not independent, state.

In October 1958 General de Gaulle was unable to overcome this
difficulty, although one does not dare blame him. Could he have
conceded the minimum demanded by the F.L.N. without provoking
a revolt by the French soldiers and citizens of Algeria? Strong in
his prestige and in his triumph at the polls, could he have imposed
on the "May factions" what Pflimlin had been accused of having
the vague intention of doing? On a personal basis, this observer

would give a positive answer to these questions, but he cannot offer proof for such an answer.

Whatever the truth may be, the move to compromise with the F.L.N. failed, and the character of the November elections was altered. Political leaders from France, who were hoping to offer themselves with liberal campaign slogans, saw that such an attempt was impossible. Among the Moslems no moderate nationalist candidate came forward. The F.L.N. had been unable to prevent the Moslems from voting in large numbers on September 28, but it had supplied proof as planned that the Moslems who were prepared to run for office in spite of the disapproval of the F.L.N. were either too "French" or too closely linked with the French army to have any representative value. It was either the French army or the F.L.N.; the two stood face to face again, with any arbitration momentarily out of the question, any go-between thrust aside.

In one way General de Gaulle made the search for a negotiated settlement more difficult. Whatever one may think of the elections, the fact is that the seventy-one Algerian deputies are logically the "valid interlocutors" with whom any further progress must be achieved. The army feels morally committed to these delegates, who represent nobody in the eyes of the Algerian nationalists. Since it has been admitted that all French overseas territories have a right to independence, the only argument justifying the continuation of the present-day policy is that Algeria should remain an integral part of the national domain. In order for Algeria not be to like Guinea, she must be like Brittany. Between Guinea and Brittany only Article 72 of the Constitution opens a middle way: a group of *départements* could be subject to an administration partially different from that of the rest of the country.

General de Gaulle has at the same time refused to accept the formula of integration, and has begun to put it into effect at the political level, while depriving it of any ideological foundation. Why should not Algerians have the same rights as Tunisians or Guineans? In fact, the French government has solid reasons for not giving up its sovereignty across the Mediterranean. The majority of Algerian Europeans would never consent to live under an Algerian republic. Without the European minority the Algerian masses would know a still worse fate, because the fragile structure of modern economy would collapse. Algeria is the indispensable southern base of the defense of western Europe; it is the access to the oil of the Sahara. One can plead that necessity is more pressing than any kind of ideology.

It remains to be seen how long and at what price France will manage to resist the implications of her own philosophy. Not that the F.L.N. is in a position to win: never has a guerrilla force defeated a large army, and the rebellion is on the wane compared with a year ago. The closing of the borders is more effective; the so-called "army of liberation" lacks munitions and has had to stop operating in large detachments. It is further, in 1959, from the phase Mao Tse-Tung called the generalized counteroffensive than it was in 1957, but neither is it on the brink of submission unless there should be a sudden collapse of morale.

Are the two sides resigned or unflinchingly committed to a struggle to the end? Judging by the facts, the observer should come to this pessimistic conclusion. But revolutionary wars are always as much psychological as they are physical. Before 1958 the F.L.N. counted on the weakness of the Fourth Republic, on the accession some day or other of a government ready to concede what the preceding one had refused. General de Gaulle is in for seven years, and, in spite of the elections, the Algerian nationalists have a confidence in him they never gave Guy Mollet or any of the leaders of the Fourth Republic.

*   *   *

The Constitution of France, the Constitution of the Community, elections in Algeria—these do not exhaust the list of achievements of the interim government between the Fourth and Fifth Republics. Like many others since 1789, the regime founded by General de Gaulle began in a fever heat of reforms: legal, administrative, economic, financial, educational. A large part of this legislation is neither conservative nor radical, neither reactionary nor progressive. Some laws embody plans which had been moldering for years in ministers' files. Others realize reforms which specialists or enlightened opinion had been hoping for. For example, a young and able minister, Sudreau, took some of the measures destined to solve the permanent housing shortage. Also, the legal reform, questionable on many points, does answer the obvious need to change the plan of the judiciary, which had been fixed for a century and a half, and to adapt it to demographic and economic changes.

Whatever the merits of the interregnum, one could not say that the semirevolutionary period, which began with the war in Algeria and the collapse of the Fourth Republic, is over. Most surely, General de Gaulle, called to power by the Algerian crowds and generals, has twice been approved by plebiscite of the French people. The result of the referendum, if not the percentage of *oui* votes (80 per cent), was predictable and predicted. A majority of *nons* would have included both Communists and non-Communists, and would not have come up with any government majority except a Popular Front, a contingency most of the non-Communist opposition rejected. There was no need to fall back on the threat of the paratroopers: political leaders and plain citizens knew that the parties could agree neither to go on with the war in Algeria nor to make peace. The nation, like the deputies, united to put its fate in the hands of a man who was known to be disinterested, who respected the laws and was devoted to his country, but whose own ideas were not well known.

The French Republic, like the Roman Republic, from time to time needs a dictator to impose reforms long put off because of the resistance of private interests, and to lead the country out of stalemate. Clemenceau in 1917 and Poincaré in 1925 were dictators within the parliamentary system. The Bonapartes twice took advantage of circumstances to build empires. General de Gaulle has too much respect for law to contemplate the possibility of a *coup d'état;* he was too hostile to the Fourth Republic to stay within the framework of the regime.

The French always answered *oui* to the referendum-plebiscites of

Napoleon III because they do not despise the combination of democratic ideas and personal power. Louis Napoleon's saying was that
"the nature of democracy is to become personified in one man." In
September 1958, so many questions were being asked simultaneously
that every one was inclined to answer *oui* to one or another of them.
Whoever did not like the Constitution could not deny the incontest-
able fact that the General had more chances than anyone else to get
the French and the F.L.N. to accept a compromise solution. The
non-Communist left found an additional reason for voting *oui* in the
section of the Constitution on the Community.

Never had General de Gaulle's popularity been as great as at the
time of the elections at the end of November 1958. He had given
the French both the feeling that they were being governed and the
assurance that liberties would be respected. Parliament, that English
institution, has always been less popular in France than the Republic
or democracy, undefinable but glorious. No one missed the Chamber
of Deputies and no one feared the dictator.

The General's popularity had much to do with the triumph of the
U.N.R., a party which was improvised during the weeks just before
the elections and which regrouped various Gaullist associations.
Aided by the electoral system, the party, which on the first ballot
obtained fewer votes than the Communists, elected some two hundred deputies on the second ballot, most of them former partisans
of the R.P.F. The venture of the R.P.F., which had come to such
a pitiful end in 1952-53, made a comeback in 1958; the Gaullist
party dominated the first legislature of the Fifth Republic.

In appearance the new regime is stable, since the President of the
Republic, elected by 80 per cent of the electoral college, has to deal
with an Assembly whose majority was elected in his name. But a
regime dependent upon one man as much as the Fifth Republic
depends upon General de Gaulle is, fundamentally, in a precarious
position. And one suspects that the President of the Republic hoped
that the Chamber would not present such a distorted image of French
opinion.

During the first phase, the President of the Republic will easily impose his decisions on the Prime Minister and the Chamber of Deputies on the subjects he holds dear: Algeria, foreign affairs, the army. The fidelity of the Prime Minister, Michel Debré, to the General has never failed and will not fail. But the fact still remains that the U.N.R. and the Algerian deputies and their true leader, Jacques Soustelle, will not necessarily bow to General de Gaulle one or two years from now. In time the founder of the Fifth Republic will perhaps not be its master.

For that matter, the left-wing opposition, which before September 28, 1958, denounced the excessive powers given the President of the Republic, has, since the third of December, reversed its position: it is happy that General de Gaulle is in a position to control the "Ultra" Assembly, and even to impose liberal measures in Algeria.

A forecast is all the more impossible since the war in Algeria continues and France's obligations are still so heavy. To the responsibilities of the Community, of the pacification and development of Algeria, the Gaullist Republic adds atomic and social ambitions at home. French governments, in the twentieth century, have fallen less because of their enemies than because of their inconsistencies and their failures. The Fifth Republic, at its birth, has no enemies to dread, but it has not overcome its own inconsistencies or solved France's problems.

VI ❧

ADJUSTMENT TO THE WORLD

THE crisis in France is not separable from the crisis in Europe, and the latter dates from 1914. Not one of the great powers of half a century ago avoided the maelstrom of history; each emerged deeply transformed. The Ottoman Empire disappeared and the Turkish nation was created. The Austro-Hungarian Empire broke up into national states. The empire of the Tsars became the Union of Soviet Socialist Republics, larger and stronger than the empire it succeeded and incomparably more tyrannical, although it professes the ideal of universal freedom. The empire of Wilhelm II is no longer, and the Reich itself is cut into two pieces, of which one is a satellite of the Soviet Union and the other a Western democracy. The kingdom of Savoy no longer exists, and Italy has found provisory peace in a parliamentary republic threatened on the left by the Communist Party and a progressive Socialist Party, on the right by the partisans of the monarchy and the survivors of Fascism. The tumultuous vicissitudes of French politics are also a tribute paid to the demons of the times.

At the beginning of the century legitimacy was still half traditional in central Europe and even more so in eastern Europe. Territories had been assembled by sovereigns, by random conquests, or by marriages. The rights of nationality were beginning to be recognized, and citizens were electing representatives, but the heir of kings and emperors was still the symbolic and partially effective guardian of power in Berlin, Vienna, or Budapest. He was its incarnation in Saint Petersburg.

The collapse of thrones after the war of 1914 occasioned the multiplication of national states, a new arrangement of frontiers, and at the same time the spread of parliamentary regimes, modeled on the British and French examples. In none of the states except Czechoslovakia did this form of government succeed in taking root. In Italy democracy was swept away by the backwash of the postwar period, in Germany the depression gave the Weimar Republic its *coup de grâce*.

Of the Continental powers only France kept her institutions intact until 1940. Instability manifested itself within the regime. The two conditions apparently necessary for a Fascist mass movement—a sense of humiliation and a desire for national aggrandizement, plus social unrest verging on revolutionary violence in certain classes rebelling against proletarian ideology—never coincided in France, either after the First World War or on the eve of the Second. France had not been conquered like Germany; she was not conscious of defeat like Italy. She had overthrown her hereditary monarchy a century and a half earlier and forged her unity during centuries of history.

Beginning in the 1930's, the Republic was threatened less by the number or zeal of Communists and Fascists than by the adversities the country suffered. The prolonged depression, which lasted nearly ten years, exasperated public opinion. The rise of Hitler's Germany, the mounting dangers, the feeling that the Great War had been fought and won in vain, stirred up a bitterness spontaneously expressed by blaming everything on the government. France lay between Great Britain, where parliamentary democracy was scarcely questioned, and the Continental states, where it was proving incapable of operating with success. The forces which came into play during occupation had seemed incapable of destroying the democratic regime in normal times. Conservatives of the first Vichy crew, high officials with technocratic tendencies, National Socialists or Fascists of Parisian collaborationist circles, all had one common feature: they could obtain but feeble or ridiculously small support through universal suffrage.

In the Fourth Republic the number of votes cast for candidates hostile to the constitutional system increased enormously as compared with the prewar period. But Communist voters, if one assumes that they were opposed to parliamentary democracy, were even more hostile to the idea of right-wing authoritarianism. Poujadist voters hated the technicians and technocrats whose power would be enhanced by Fascism or a regime à la Franco.

After the great strikes in 1948, the Communist Party gradually lost its power to enlist the support of workers for purely political objectives. The Poujadists were capable of anti-tax demonstrations but not revolution. The Fourth Republic was weakened by extremist votes and lacked the strength of a unanimously accepted legitimacy, but it was imperiled most of all by its very nature and by the general course of events.

Parliamentary democracy, although never universally accepted, has nonetheless never been attacked in this century by an enemy capable of mobilizing the masses. On the right, the attitude toward the Republic among many conservatives was one of resignation rather than support. Strongly represented in the salons and the academies, but with little influence on election day, they dreamed of restoring the monarchy or the corporate state. Fascists and National Socialists were mere cliques. The Communists constitute a kind of counterstate, but they live in a climate of perpetual ambiguity. Acting on orders of a foreign government, they have gained popularity by participation in movements (Popular Front, Resistance) where their slogans happened to coincide with those of French patriotism. Antiparliamentarianism has prevailed only during national disasters, either real or fictitious.

*   *   *

Political instability, sometimes within the Republic, sometimes affecting the constitutional order itself, is the immediately apparent peculiarity of twentieth-century France. But this instability, which is partly a product of history and of French temperament, is also explained by the basic contrast between France's influence in Europe and Europe's on the world, and the obligations which France has set for herself or which circumstances and her allies have imposed upon her.

The decline of French industrial and numerical power began in the nineteenth century. The most populous country in Europe except Russia in 1830, France was overtaken by the countries forming the German Empire after 1860, and dropped to fourth below Austria-Hungary about 1890. The French population increased by ten million between 1811 and 1911. In half a century, from 1860 to 1911, the population of England grew more than sixteen million, Germany's nearly thirty million.

The changes typical of modern civilization, urbanization, and industrialization took place more slowly in France than in the other major countries, her allies or rivals. In France in 1911, over 55 per cent of the population was rural; in Germany it was no more than 53 per cent in 1890, 40 per cent in 1910.

Of this relatively diminished population, a smaller population than in Germany or Great Britain made its living from industry and from the sectors of industry which are the basis of economic and military power. In a half-century, from 1866 to 1906, the proportion of the working class engaged in industry and transportation increased only from 30.7 per cent to 34.9 per cent. The number of French laborers employed in industry in 1906 was slightly below the figure for industrial labor in Germany in 1882 and in England in 1891. The proportion of industrial population was 30.2 per cent in France (1906), 52.4 per cent in England (1911), and 37.2 per cent in Germany (1907).

Employment in mining, metallurgy, and the chemical and construction industries was proportionally lower than in England and Germany. This group employed 19.8 per cent of industrial manpower in France (1906), 28 per cent in England (1911), and 29 per cent in Germany (1907). On the other hand, the group including textiles and related activities and the food industries employed 47 per cent of industrial manpower in France, 40.5 per cent in England, and 34.5 per cent in Germany at the same dates as above.[1]

Another symptom of French resistance to capitalist industrialization appears in the relatively low number of wage earners and the relatively high number of non-wage earners—that is, craftsmen, proprietors, and entrepreneurs. Wage earners made up 58.4 per cent of industrial employment in France (1906), compared to 81.3 per cent in Germany (1907); in commerce and transportation the French and German percentages are 43.4 and 63.1, in the whole economy 45.5 against 56.6, and in the nonagricultural sectors 56.8 versus 66.9.[2]

It is not our purpose to try to discover why French families voluntarily had fewer children half a century or more earlier than in other European countries, or what causes contributed to the slackening of the pace of industrialization. Historians and economists have offered many explanations; the scarcity of coal deposits at a time when heavy industries were settling near the coal mines, the family-type structure of many industrial enterprises, failure to adapt mental attitudes and legislation to industrial growth, state protection of agriculture and traditional customs, et cetera. The brute fact alone interests us: the leading industrial power on the Continent in 1850, France was greatly outdistanced both absolutely and relatively a half-century later by Germany.

France has known three favorable periods during the twentieth century. From 1900 to 1913, as we have seen, per-capita industrial development was faster than in the rest of Europe, even Germany, but the latter's lead continued to increase in absolute terms (annual cast-iron production in France increased from 2,540,000 tons in

---

[1] Here are the comparisons in index form:

	France	England	Germany
All industry	100	154	180
Group I	100	218	260
Group II	100	132	131

[2] These figures are borrowed from Pommera, Coquet and Laurat, eds., *Grandeur et déclin de la France* (Paris, 1946).

1896–1900 to 3,590,000 in 1907 and 5,207,000 tons in 1913; during the same period German production went from 7,425,000 tons to 11,-390,000 and 16,764,000). From 1919 to 1929, progress in France was both absolutely and relatively superior to progress in Europe generally and in Germany in particular. In 1929 France produced more cast iron than England (10,362,000 tons as compared to 7,711,000) and almost as much steel (9,716,000 tons against 9,791,000). Finally, progress was again rapid from 1946 to 1958, and particularly from 1949 to 1958, especially if calculated in terms of per-capita income or worker productivity.

Unfortunately, these three prosperous periods were cut short not only by the two wars and their attendant devastations, but by the 1931–39 depression, by the end of which the index of industrial production was some twenty points lower than in 1929, whereas in the leading countries it was twenty to twenty-five points above that level. In 1938, metallurgic production was 35 per cent below the 1929 level, and in mechanical engineering the drop was 30 per cent.

While industry was going through these alternate stages— alternations connected with international developments but accentuated in France—the declining birth rate continued until just before the Second World War. The reversal of the trend began during the years of occupation, unnoticed because of the circumstances. It suddenly became apparent in 1946 and has continued since then. There are more than 800,000 youths of draft age. There were about 600,000 before the war. The renewal of generations is assured from now on. There will be an increase of 150,000 in manpower available for the labor market three years from now. If France can then maintain the rate of industrial growth of recent years, the prospects of development and prosperity are brilliant.

To hold the place she wanted in diplomacy, France, smaller in population and less industrialized than her enemy, Germany, and her ally, Great Britain, had to put forth efforts and consent to sacrifices out of proportion with those of the other European nations. Are the human losses in war responsible for the lower national vitality, as has sometimes been alleged? Have the sacrificed generations stripped the nation of those who would have been its leaders and inspirers? Is the reverse natural selection of modern warfare responsible for the stagnation of the 1930's and the collapse in 1940? I plead guilty of skepticism toward this common interpretation. In a few scientific disciplines the death of youths who were to take the lead has had lasting consequences. But the contrast with the two interwar decades is too abrupt for the depression of the 1930's to be attributed to the deaths of the heroes. By 1929, the ruins had been restored and, in spite of inflation, industrial progress was more than respectable.

The disproportion between France's own resources and her international role, which had appeared during the war in the form of losses proportionally higher than those of her allies and adversaries, manifested itself between the two wars by a policy the outer world thought to be sometimes aggressive, at other times weak, but which was essentially conservative. France, conscious of the precariousness of a victory won with the help of a vast coalition which had dissolved even before hostilities had ended, tried to maintain the *status quo*. This conservative policy, which may appear reasonable in retrospect, was not supported by either Great Britain or the United States. The former, obsessed by old recollections, took offense at French supremacy when she should have been dreading its collapse. The United States, disappointed in the results of victory, fell back on one strand of its tradition and attempted to avoid further involvement in Old World quarrels. France found herself alone, except for the support of the small states born of the disintegration of the Austro-Hungarian Empire, charged with the enormous task of preserving the order of the Versailles Treaty, which the two strongest Continental powers, Germany and Russia, considered contrary to their interests. Disarmament of the Reich and demilitarization of the Rhineland were the foundations of peace. The French leaders were less unaware than the British leaders. But had they the means, assuming they had the desire, to impose indefinitely by armed force the disarmament of a great state?

People were astonished at the blend of defeatism and conservatism, of obstinate refusal and sudden abandon, which characterized our diplomacy between the two wars. As usual they blamed the government. Never had a regime been given a mission more contrary to its nature: the bourgeois republic had to pledge a magnitude of purpose unrelated to the actual balance of power. A France with a declining population, half-industrialized, attempted first to prevent the military resurgence of Germany, and then to control the Third Reich strengthened by conquest.

After 1919 the French had (and indeed could have) but one desire: to conserve the fruits of a victory dearly paid for, to preserve a European order which, miraculously, weakened the "hereditary enemy"—to arrest history, as has been said. What could history bring that would not be a loss to a country which by accident was recovering its ascendancy in Europe and keeping a vast overseas empire?

Should France have strained her will, prepared for battle, if war became inevitable, in order to safeguard her heritage? It seems to me psychologically understandable that the nation should have been constantly divided, incapable of choosing between a sincere attempt at reconciliation with her former enemy and an inflexible determination to defend the treaty which invested her with a precarious supremacy, or that she was still more unable to choose between two alternatives when Hitler came to power. Before 1914 the General Staff was Bergsonian and believed in the virtues of an all-out offensive. Before 1939 it believed in the unbroken line, in the superiority of defense. The two doctrines also symbolize France's outlook on the world and the future. If one recalls that the war of 1939 came at the end of an economic depression, which was accompanied by an almost constant state of political crisis, the collapse of 1940 is more easily understood.

This collapse was, first and foremost, a military defeat, caused by the failure to adapt the machinery of war to modern warfare. Throughout history other nations have suffered similar disasters.

Even a state dedicated to warfare, like Prussia, experienced Jena. Democracy was not to be blamed for Crécy and Agincourt. The intellectual rigidity we have seen so often in all spheres of action was behind the first reverses, in 1914 as well as in 1940. The leaders had accepted a theory and forgotten certain facts. When the theory was refuted by the facts in 1914, the army succeeded in a miraculous recovery on the Marne. Recovery was technically more difficult in 1940 because the means of exploiting initial successes had been so greatly increased. But the French nation was also no longer welded together by a unanimous will; France was doubtful about herself, her cause, her government, and her future.

After the Second World War France went through another mutation. Too costly a victory in 1918 had inspired anxious conservatism in the face of history. But now a disaster followed by four years of occupation and participation in the final triumph created an entirely different atmosphere. The rise in the birth rate is partly explained by this psychological change. The ambition for economic development at any price is another expression of the new state of mind. Aspiring not to lose their place in the world, Frenchmen had dreamed, between the wars, of stopping history. Now they are dreaming of developing their resources commensurate with their ambitions. Progress at home and colonial wars in Asia and Africa are perhaps contradictory expressions of the same impulse.

The French colonial empire was won, for the most part, in the last century, under the Third Republic (it covered 373,000 square miles in 1875, 4,080,000 in 1914: of a population of 56,000,000, 50,000,-000 lived in areas conquered after 1875). In 1914 France was the second colonial power in the world, immediately following Great Britain. The empire held only a modest place in the foreign commerce of the homeland (9.9 per cent of the imports, 14.2 per cent of the exports), even more modest in capital investment. Next to Great Britain, in the last century and at the beginning of the present one, France was the world's banker. On the eve of the war, French investments abroad were estimated, by the services of the League of Nations, to be between 52 and 60 billion francs, by other experts at

45 billion.[3] But of 45 billion francs, 30 were invested in Europe, more than a third of it in Russia, and of about 15 billion francs invested in Asia, Africa, and America, about 4 billion francs were in the French colonies, which had, then, received less than 10 per cent of the capital invested by the French outside the country by 1913.

Between the wars, the share of the empire in French exports slowly increased, going from 14 per cent in 1923 to 20.6 per cent in 1930, while the share of French imports from the empire was steady at around 12 per cent. The percentages increased with and because of the depression. The empire absorbed an increased share of French exports because exports to foreign countries diminished in volume and also in value.[4] In the last years before the war the fraction diminished somewhat and fell back to about 27 per cent of the total. Public opinion became conscious of the usefulness of the empire as a protected market in case of financial crisis, though it did not recognize clearly that such an expedient temporarily attenuated the consequences of the setback of French exports on unprotected markets without destroying them. It is only the latter which bring in the foreign currency with which to buy the raw materials and energy which territories under the French flag do not provide.

Whatever the historical interpretation one chooses to give French colonization, the fact is that as a whole the nation took only a moderate interest in it. The capitalists who are accused of having pressured governments to conquer lands and people did not represent the general consensus of their class. Everything happened as though statesmen were invoking necessities which bankers and industrialists for the most part were bent on ignoring, as though the military were looking for glory and "cannon fodder," as though France found in it a sort of vain gratification and a few Frenchmen the chance to convert souls, exploit resources, seek adventure, or make quick profits from untapped nature.

If French leaders and public opinion refused to admit after the

[3] English foreign investments were twice as much, Germany's a third less.
[4] Exports to the empire diminished by 37 per cent between 1929 and 1933, foreign exports 69 per cent. The empire's share thus increased from 18.8 per cent to 32.4 per cent.

Second World War that the colonial balance sheet was usually in the red, if the financial arguments for withdrawal were still without weight, it was because the empire had never been an economic enterprise. Ideals, glory, power, had at one time or another determined national interest; rarely had policy been determined by commercial considerations. The nation had answered the call of the crusader or conqueror, not the so-called practical reasoning of banker and trader. The dream was to transform the empire into an overseas France—a dream whose realization was not promoted by the more or less inevitable conduct of the pioneers or settlers in North and Black Africa even when their behavior did not turn it into a bitter mockery.

Just after the Second World War France had fewer material resources than at any time since *"l'année terrible."* [5] General de Gaulle ordered France to play a role commensurate not with her means, but with his own conceptions of her grandeur. The parliamentarians who followed him, contrary to all the legendary accounts, took over without abandoning the policy of greatness. Georges Bidault, who has been unjustly accused of being taken in tow by Washington, more often led than followed the State Department. He wanted to continue the struggle in Indochina when President Eisenhower was signing the Korean armistice, and tried to get the American air force to intervene to save the garrison of Dien Bien Phu. Bidault's error was not that he acted as governor of a satellite of the United States but that he adopted objectives without considering the possibilities. The famous saying that "the word 'impossible' is not French" became the slogan of a diplomacy which its advocate did not consider condemned merely by failure. Never has intellectual rigidity assumed a more tragically anachronistic form: to stay in Asia when Great Britain and Holland were withdrawing, to unite erstwhile enemies in Europe, to save the sovereignty of France in Africa. The triple ambition was grandiose. To aim at anything less

---

[5] July 1870 to May 1871, the year of the Franco-Prussian War. *L'Année terrible* is the title of a collection of poems on this period by Victor Hugo. (L.E.)

was to give up entirely. Because one had yielded at Munich without having fought and at Compiègne without having exhausted all means of fighting, any kind of retreat became the symbol of the spirit of surrender, and the refusal to make any concession the symbol of the spirit of resistance. But to stubbornly oppose the demands of the nationalists—was that to be faithful to the *Résistants* who wanted to free France from foreign occupation?

After 1871, France had been obsessed with the blue line of the Vosges and had opened up for those who would have wearied of long waiting a career of adventure and glory in Africa. The double hope of revenge and compensation was fulfilled in 1918. France then had nothing left to hope for except that "things might last." After 1945 everything had to be rebuilt; France had to adjust to a world which had been transformed.

* * *

For France this adjustment had a triple aspect: economic, diplomatic and imperial. For a hundred years everything had gone along as though the country had offered a blunt resistance to industrial civilization. Public opinion deplored the rural exodus instead of regretting the slow pace of industrialization, and denounced the soulless city and the giant factories, sang of the nobility of the craftsman, the virtues of those who were independent, whether peasants, businessmen, or manufacturers, without realizing that traditional ways of life and labor, when they become out of date, lose their virtues and that industry, whatever the human cost, is in this century the prerequisite for prosperity and power. After 1945, administrators, government officials, manufacturers, and economists were all firmly resolved to modernize the whole country. The attitude of the ordinary citizen toward the factory, technical innovations, and the future had changed. The Monnet Plan and the planning and production commissions were the outward expressions or instruments of this will for modernization. Not without mistakes, dissensions, imperfections, are the results there, and they are respectable. Yearly increases in production of 7 and 8 per cent, recurring for several years in succession, prove, if need be, that this time France is on its way.

But another kind of adjustment, more difficult in spite of appearances, was demanded. In the economy it was enough to substitute the ideal of growth for that of the pseudo-balance between agriculture and industry. In diplomacy the enemy had to be accepted as a friend, yesterday's ally recognized as tomorrow's enemy, and it was necessary to resign oneself to being no longer a great power. I do not know what the mass of plain citizens thought. I do know that the politicians, like the intellectuals, have not easily reconciled themselves to the fate that circumstances were imposing on them. Both groups are divided, each political faction, each school of thought, seeking to satisfy to some extent French nationalism and her aspiration to grandeur.

Everyone reproached everybody else for accepting a subordinate position for France. The Communist Party was the agent of an "alien nationalism"; advocates of the North Atlantic Pact were lowering France to the status of a satellite of the United States; the "Europeans" were consenting to see France swallowed up in a supranational organization; those who proposed reconciliation with North African nationalism were "defeatists," doctrinaires of surrender. Each, as seen by the other, was not a good Frenchman; each one justified himself with patriotic argument.

The Communists never tired of calling for French independence, compromised [they said] by the North Atlantic Pact; the progressives reproached the supporters of NATO with "following" the United States and not finding a properly French policy. Nor did the "Europeans" hesitate to soothe hearts with the old song, rejuvenated by new hopes: Europe, if not France, would be a third Great Power, able to talk on an equal basis with the two giants. The old Continent, united in one State, would not be outclassed by any continent-state.

Economic adjustment is well on its way in spite of the obstacles it is meeting. The intellectual conversion has at any rate been accom-

ADJUSTMENT TO THE WORLD

plished: the nature, the means, the demands of industrial civilization have been understood and accepted by the governing class. The diplomatic adjustment, which is, by its nature, unending, is also in progress. The Fourth Republic, all things considered, had an honorable share in the main episodes of postwar international politics: the North Atlantic Pact, Franco-German reconciliation, European Union.

To be sure, the diplomacy of the Fourth Republic was entirely satisfactory to no one. But how could it have satisfied one sect without arousing the violent opposition of the other? One puts in the debit column what was caused by the quarrels of the politicians and the intellectual rigidity of each faction. Seventy-five per cent of Frenchmen were, in one way or another, in favor of a close cooperation between western European countries, but a third or half of them opposed any transfer of sovereignty. Either one watered down the European plan in order to make it acceptable to everybody, in which case the advocates of a federal Europe denounced the nation for acting as a brake on progress, or one suggested setting up a federated state, and then the nationalists, not opposed to cooperation but hostile to a federation, burst into a storm. The second term of the alternative was put to the test with the European Defense Community, which occasioned a great debate in the true French style, passionate, theoretical, and confused. The Common Market returned to the first alternative and the parliamentary obstacles were overcome.

In the same way, a majority of Frenchmen was finally resigned to the rearming of yesterday's enemy. But this majority melted away as soon as the question of method came up. Should it be rearmament within the framework of an European army or within NATO? It was likely that, of the two procedures, the later one submitted for the consent of the Assembly would be the choice. The satisfaction of resisting American pressure was not the least reason for voting against the E.D.C.

In foreign relations, the Fourth Republic finally accomplished what depended on it for success: getting the country to accept a reconciliation with Germany and the necessity of an Atlantic alliance, and undertaking the task of European unity. It could be observed that the circumstances hardly left any choice. Circumstances were certainly compelling, but the number of those in France who clamor for independent diplomacy or dream of reviving the Franco-Soviet treaty is so great that the advocate of the Atlantic alliance is justified in finding one merit of the Fourth Republic in a diplomacy which did not revolt against reality.

It was in the empire that the Fourth Republic failed. It is in relation to empire that the very meaning of what we call adjustment to the world of today is disputed. In one way or another all Frenchmen want their country to share fully in industrial civilization. All—except the Communists—accept cooperation with Western Germany within the European and Atlantic communities, but Frenchmen are still divided on Algeria and anticolonialism, about what has happened in the last ten years and about what might have happened.

Typical Anglo-Saxon anticolonialism is based on two arguments, or rather on two facts. The colonial economic balance sheet has, during most of the time, shown a loss; the more progress the colonies make, the more the minorities who speak for them claim independence. Whence comes an argument which is, so to speak, the synthesis of these two and which is found clearly expressed in one of Mr. Myrdal's last books.

In the dependencies which still linger, the military and other expenses needed to maintain the regime, the costs and losses caused by the popular revolts, and the financial burden of necessary social reforms and investments in economic development take the profitability out of the colonial system and make it instead increasingly a liability to the metropolitan countries. . . When the profitability of the system is gradually lost and it stands out as an increasingly expensive political luxury, the colonial system is doomed and the national ideologies will be readjusted accordingly.[6]

---

[6] Gunnar Myrdal, *Rich Lands and Poor: The Road to World Prosperity* (New York, 1957), p. 61 [published in England under the title of *Economic Theory and Under-Developed Regions,* pp. 60–61].

This expresses an optimism which the Algerian tragedy suffices to belie.

The balance sheet of the colonies becomes negative for the colonial powers to the extent that the burden of social or economic investment increases. The mother countries are no longer in quest of investment for their capital; they all lack the capital to meet their own needs. They no longer have to look for outlets for manufactured goods—both developed and underdeveloped countries are clamoring for them; the same is true for consumer goods—in industrialized countries the increased income of the masses absorbs them. They are in need of raw materials, but they can acquire them even when they have given up colonial sovereignty. Henceforth, the economic value of a colony increases the more its subsoil conceals raw materials and the fewer men its topsoil supports. A desert producing millions of tons of crude oil—such is the ideal colony of the twentieth century.

The discovery of oil in the Sahara has belatedly given France the "ideal colony" of our time, though the millions of Algerians who live between the desert and the coast radically modify the situation. The discovery of oil has furnished an economic justification for an ambition which predated it, and which has recourse to bad arguments when good ones are lacking (some do not hesitate to assert that Algeria is indispensable to French laborers, who would be idle so many days a year if the tricolor were lowered across the Mediterranean). French national aspirations have not adjusted to the present-day balance sheet of colonial domination primarily because the empire had never been thought of as an economic enterprise.

The more the empire was the luxury of a wealthy country or a work of idealism or vanity, the more France (or those speaking for her) refused to surrender it at the time when she was left humiliated by the defeat of 1940 and by the loss of prestige brought on by the replacement of a European by a world-wide diplomacy.

At the time when French prestige was wounded, the empire was subjected to a triple attack: the attack of the peoples themselves, that of the Soviet Union and its propaganda, and the ideological (and at times political) attack of the United States. President Roosevelt was consciously, resolutely hostile to the British and French empires (he was not yet hostile to the Soviet empire). While delivering a hundred million people of Europe to Soviet domination he wanted to free Africans and Asians from European domination. In Indochina the American authorities favored Ho Chi Minh and opposed the French for months after the Japanese surrender.

Granted, colonization had created vested interests, the interests of the governing officials or those of businessmen. Vested interests defended themselves as best they could, and their spokesmen accused politicians or journalists who favored an understanding with the nationalists of "defeatism" or "abandonment." But in Morocco, where the decision was made that was to settle the fate of all North Africa, the directors of the banks and large companies were split; some of them favored negotiation with the Sultan and the Istiqlal, while others wanted to keep the protectorate just as it was or to select as interlocutors those who were traditional friends of France. Only in Algeria was there unanimity, or near-unanimity, for resistance, and those playing the leading parts, especially the big vineyard owners, enriched by the billions of francs made in 1956 and 1957, had the support of the mass of the Europeans established across the Mediterranean in the campaign launched with enormous means to convince the homeland. But the resistance of the vested interests would not have been so hard to overcome in Indochina and Algeria if a significant number of politicians, army men, and plain citizens had not, for entirely different reasons, upheld the same theses.

The army, in Asia and even more in North Africa, was defending its achievements; it was perhaps seeking a compensation for the disaster of 1940; it was trying to preserve the fortunes of the empire—that is, from its point of view, the splendor of France. The chain of command, as well as public opinion, still clung to time-honored notions: the loss of empires brings on the decadence of the mother countries, the surrender of sovereignty leaves nothing remaining of the colonial achievement, the winning of independence by colonies indicates the defeat of imperial power, and so on.

Whatever one's own preferences may be, why should this state of mind, which was that of all conquerors for thousands of years, be shameful? Anticolonialist orthodoxy is either the ideology of a people who have a surplus of space available, or of an insular and commercial nation who can strike a balance and act according to circumstances.

French colonization was military, peasant, Roman. As an ideal its object was to convert, if not souls to Christ, at least men to France and her civilization. The empire was a thing of glory, the foundation of a world power; that it should also be a source of profit was declared in order to convince the "shopkeepers" (there are some everywhere), but that it might cease being a source of profit and become a burden was not a valid reason for giving it up. One never pays too dearly for the honor of reigning.

Anachronism? Yes, unquestionably, this state of mind belongs to another era. On the level of politics events have spoken a clear language. But even after the event the question is still debatable. The impatience with which the United States has urged the liquidation of the European empires will perhaps appear, too, in retrospect, to have been a tragedy of history.

The United States could easily support a population of three hundred million without giving up the methods of extensive agriculture, with its low yield per acre and high yield per laborer. Europeans live in a confined space and (the French excepted, whose soil could easily support some tens of millions more) they must purchase abroad the food needed for an eventual surplus population (even now the British and the Western Germans import half and a third, respectively, of their food). In the same way, European factories depend on importation of raw materials. By losing their military positions around the world, Europeans lose, in a way, their autonomy. The supply of food for men and machines is no longer assured by the protection of the flag, the Royal Navy, or the Colonial Office, but is subject to the caprices of weak governments moved by passion or resentment rather than economic considerations.

Since the sources of supply are no longer under the sovereign control of a Western state, Europe must bargain as best it can. The United States is in a less precarious position; it can, if necessary, take what others would be tempted to refuse; it is, because of the very volume of its purchases, better able to dictate its conditions than the Europeans.

Problematic with regard to Europe, the policy of "decolonization" is also problematic with regard to the peoples of Asia and Africa. Everything depends on their capacity to reach, after becoming independent, the goal they all have in mind: that is, participation in technical civilization. Success in this, depending on the area, is either likely or unlikely.

Just after the war three phenomena appeared simultaneously. They were the realization that colonial rule is not profitable, the weakness of the European mother countries, and the strong world-wide support given the anticolonial theories of the United States and the Soviet Union. If expediency was to be the basis for action, the lesson to be learned was clear and its application obvious. But if principles were to be considered, the coincidence of these three phenomena gave rise to contradictory interpretations. To yield to anticolonialist sermonizing was to obey, as at Munich, as in 1940, the spirit of surrender, to abandon in midstream peoples for whom one had become responsible, in short, to act as a satellite of the United States. In practical politics this might have been a reason to say *yes,* but in reasoning by theories and emotions it became a motive for saying *no.*

Logically it would have been preferable to consent or refuse, depending on the circumstances, to set up a timetable for the progression toward independence, for transitions and terms acceptable to everybody. In fact, the *yes* is infectious, and the liberation of the colored races is not being carried out any more in conformity with the wishes of men of good will than was their conquest. The agents of revolt, primarily Westernized intellectuals, are impatient to replace yesterday's masters, alleging that they put freedom above bread, if necessary (but the masses—not they—would be deprived of bread).

The end of colonialism is actually quite likely in many places to worsen the living conditions of the former colonial peoples, at least in the immediate future.

The danger of conflict between political liberation and economic growth is all the greater the fewer the native administrators and the more important the sectors of national life controlled by the erstwhile masters. In this sense, the French protectorates were the least prepared for putting the theory of anticolonialism into practice. Overnight, French investment of capital was reduced or stopped entirely; aid from France was suspended at a time when French specialists remained more indispensable than ever. What can be done when the aspiration of the elite for independence cannot be satisfied without deceiving the hope of the people for improved conditions?

The revolt against Europe is not calmed by the mere juridico-military retreat of the imperial power. A government which maintains overcordial relations with it or with the West becomes suspect in the eyes of the nationalists of Asia or Africa. The acquisition of independence on the part of underdeveloped countries puts into motion a dialectic which leads to neutrality, then to positive neutralism, sometimes ending in Communism. In the first phase the demand is for political sovereignty, but the pretense is to safeguard economic cooperation, and the appeal is made for foreign capital. Soon that becomes suspect, especially when it is invested in oil. After political independence comes the desire for economic independence, which is compromised either by the presence of big international corporations or by the domination of some wealthy country or group of wealthy countries, who are free to fix or manipulate the prices of primary products.

In Latin America it is the United States which is imperialistic, even though it has never sought to acquire the least territorial possession in the Roman or French sense of sovereignty. But it is the chief buyer of coffee, copper, and tin, the prices of which control the prosperity of Brazil, Chile, and Bolivia. The big oil and fruit companies are American. They exert, or can exert, influence on the governments of the weak states. How could the United States fail to appear imperialistic?

In other words, according to the reasoning of Frenchmen who reject the Anglo-Saxon doctrine, anticolonialism is only one phase of the revolt against the West. When sovereignty has disappeared, all forms of foreign influence [*la présence*], in turn, become unbearable. The revolt against the West is not to be calmed by withdrawal. Each retreat arouses new demands. Eventually the West will be only a small island of wealthy liberal societies, surrounded by other societies, some in the Soviet style, with powerful industry and a mediocre standard of living, and others which will be both weak and poverty-stricken.

The slogan of our time is not freedom; it is equality. Political equality among peoples, symbolized by anticolonialism and the independence of colonial territories, fatally multiplies the demands, if it increases the economic inequalities. Yet this has for ten years been the distinguishing feature of history. The number of independent states increases. The gap between rich and poor countries becomes wider. Anticolonialism, which tolerates this inequality or which fails to preserve the conditions indispensable for its abatement, at most complies with the short-term interest of the imperial powers. Anticolonialism may be, to use Germaine Tillion's expression, "an alibi for pauperization."

To the theory which the West considers the only acceptable one, and to the policy which our allies consider the only reasonable one, a number of French leaders, and a portion of the nation itself, have offered resistance, which is not at all mysterious if one remembers the traditional thinking of all nations, the specific character of French "colonialism," and the arguments which even today defend the thesis, now become heretical, of the retention of sovereignty. The French might have the feeling of working for the liberation of the individual and personal equality through the diffusion of Western culture just as much as by the transfer of sovereignty to a community imbued with an Islamic vision. Only one argument was decisive, one which the French are apt to pride themselves in scorning: reality. The nationalists, appealing to religion, the past, or Western values, had become strong enough to condemn the French administration to a use of force which nullified her economic and social action. Agreement with the nationalists was full of disadvantages for the French and dangers for the ex-protectorates, but it could not be avoided.

*   *   *

Most foreigners who write about France have chosen their hero and their villain. Usually the hero is Jean Monnet, because he is the man of European unity. Now a European France would no longer be the pre-eminent nation whose government, centralized to the utmost by kings, revolutionaries, and Napoleon, still keeps the nation tied up in a strait jacket of regulations and continues to deprive citizens, private associations, communes, and regions of their initiative and autonomy. The two themes of federation at the European level and decentralization within France meet in the thinking of the "Europeans," who are acclaimed by so many of our friends abroad but detested by those who returned to power in 1958 because of the war in Algeria.

Although it is hard to judge these debates without prejudice, the observer does not lack facts and arguments, not to condemn the plan of the "Europeans," but to bring out the dubious points. The army, for Continental states, is what the navy is for an island power. Would the United Kingdom have consented to put its fleet under the command of a European ministry, to transfer to a European commission certain attributes of sovereignty, the nomination of general officers, or the organization and training of troops? Why be astonished or indignant that a number of politicians in France have refused such an alienation of sovereignty, which was equivalent to doing away with France as a political unit for the benefit of a superior unit, called Europe?

Those who drew up the E.D.C. treaty, and who clung until the
end to its supranational clauses are, from the historian's viewpoint,
fully as responsible for its final failure as the nationalists who led
the campaign against the European army. The make-up of the
National Assembly and the division of public opinion being known,
the group which tried to enforce its *own* solution of German rearmament and European cooperation without compromising on essential
points inevitably set off a "great debate." In a divided country, the
refusal to compromise is no less loaded with dangers than is an
overindulgence in bargaining.

The federal state of the Six which the anti-Europeans suspected
and denounced behind the inextricable complications of the Defense
Community was in certain ways a strange conception. It included
two thirds of a divided Germany; it excluded the colonies and
protectorates subject to French rule. The Europeans were working
toward the future, but they reserved for a reunited Germany the
right to secede. The European ministry was to take charge of the
French divisions on the Continent, but the divisions of the French
Union were still to depend only on the French government. A
strange community whose obligations the two chief members accepted only conditionally—subject to review, one of them reserving until
the day of union her decision and the other her overseas possessions.

A federation among old nations, rich in glory won at each other's
expense, each of which celebrates a victory while the other ponders
a defeat, would have required not only a common enemy and a
reasonable desire to overcome the past, but a faith. The European
patriots—I mean those for whom Europe is a fatherland for which
one is ready to make the same sacrifices offered for centuries on end
to kings or nations—were only a minority who did not even dare
to confess their objectives. The European Community was an administration without a staff or commander-in-chief. It formed and
equipped the divisions later put under command of an American
general. Is it astonishing that French nationalism, comparable to
English, American, or Swiss nationalism, rebelled?

From the viewpoint of the French and Swiss Europeans, "nationalism" and the "nation state" are historically out of date, legitimate for underdeveloped countries, for peoples just emerging from the era of colonization, whose revolt against the humiliation of yesterday can be calmed only by overcompensation. For peoples who have reached maturity, nationalism is no more than the memory of a youthful emotion.

According to this interpretation of the world, nationalism would be good only for communities which are not yet nations. The Algerians have a right to nationalism because they have no national past and because they are not all even of the same race or tradition. The French, who clearly constitute a nation, have no use for a nationalism which is henceforth out of date and reactionary. That this logic—nationalism is made for populations which have not yet attained nationhood—has an element of truth in it, we will admit. But it also includes an element of paradox, which has not the excuse of being a whole truth.

Nations conscious of their past and of their will do not need to reconfirm their nationhood daily by opposing others, or to control their domestic quarrels by denouncing imperialisms, either real or imaginary. But the old nations do not on that account lose the capacity for collective exaltation; individuals keep their pride in deeds achieved together, and they aspire to the pride which the state transmits mythically to those who obey it. The citizens of a state, whether it is Soviet, American, or French, whatever the diversity of national ideals, have not become indifferent to the power of the community.

Should the citizens of France, Italy, or Germany attain this indifference because they cannot rule like Americans or Russians and because they no longer have to fight, like the Algerians, to discover and get others to recognize their real nature? If Europeans were to become indifferent to collective power, the movement toward European unity would lose its spirit, for it too is animated by a nationalism, a European nationalism from which one hopes for a greatness and glory which the national state no longer gives.

No matter what anyone says, nations and sovereignties have not lost their meaning. The nation is the community to which one belongs more than to any other: sovereignty is the attribute of the community, mistress of herself. Nothing is more certain than that the sovereign community is only capable of action limited by the superior strength of other communities. That sovereignty, far from being an illusion, is still a major reality is sufficiently proved by the events of the last few years. Because it was a sovereign state, Egypt nationalized the Suez Canal and, although conquered on the field of battle, triumphed over Israel, France, and England, thanks to the support of all the states desirous of safeguarding the rights of states and the principles of the United Nations Charter. Because it is a sovereign state, Tunisia obtained the evacuation of French troops. When a state transfers part of its sovereignty to a higher organization, either it gives up its political essence, or it is aspiring to share in a political entity of a superior nature. Those who call themselves Europeans want to renounce the nations of France, Germany, and Italy in order to pay allegiance to a European nation as diversified as the U.S.S.R. or Switzerland, but conscious of its unity. The European state would be federal, not unitary, but it would exist only because of nationalism if nationalism is defined by the will of a group of human beings to distinguish themselves and compel recognition: in other words, by a will for collective power.

If this will for collective power does not exist, then cooperation between European states is still necessary, but federation is not. It is irritating to hear lawyers plead a good cause with bad arguments. The countries of Europe are not faced with the choice of federation or decadence. The years since the end of the war would suffice, if there were need, to prove it. The rate of growth in Germany, Italy, France—in all countries in the O.E.E.C.—has been remarkably high, perceptibly higher than in the United States since 1950. A domestic market of forty-five or fifty million is enough for most sectors of industry. The few industries (machine tools, aeronautics, atomic energy) which do not find within national limits either the necessary capital or market must make certain agreements. These would not require a political federation; nor does the latter guarantee that these agreements to cooperate and specialize would be concluded. I do not deny that Europe would be richer if it had developed within the organization of a common market. Nor do I deny that in the long run the common market speeds growth either by doing away with the marginal enterprises or by maintaining an atmosphere of competition or by favoring specialization.

I doubt, however, that the undertaking of a common market is fully justified by strictly economic considerations. Those who would be indifferent or opposed to the prospect of common activity by the Six on the world stage would at least hesitate when faced with the difficulties and risks of suppressing tariff barriers. It is in the consciousness of having a common destiny that Europeans find the ultimate reason for their choice. Or rather, it is the will to transmute this community, now under domination, into an autonomous community of action which is at the root of the European plan. The nations of the old Continent are living one and the same historical experience. Will they insist on answering the challenge of their abasement individually? Or will they unite in order to find an answer in common?

Let this be fully understood: unity, in itself, is not the answer. To survive as we know it in the continuity of values it embodies and which distinguish it, Europe must accomplish three tasks: it must resist the pressure of Soviet power (which alternates among blackmail, threat, and enticement), armed as it is with thermonuclear bombs and a Western ideology of Russo-Asiatic application; it must assure the supply of food and raw materials for its economy in a world in which it no longer has the strength to coerce its purveyors; it must maintain or establish peaceful, if not friendly, relations with underdeveloped countries, especially those which it once colonized or dominated. The method of cooperation among the countries of Europe matters less than the achievement of these tasks by the various countries, either separately or together.

Have the countries of Europe a better chance of accomplishing these things if they unite? Probably, on condition that competition inside the Common Market does not deter them from helping the countries of Asia and Africa that have recently been promoted to independence. If nationless nationalisms prevail in Africa, and if the old nations organize into a common market on the old Continent, history will go on deepening the chasm between Europeans on the one hand and Asians and Africans on the other. Now the pace at which Europeans will continue to enrich themselves matters less than the pace at which Asians and Africans will begin to make progress.

*   *   *

Of the four "greats" of Western Europe—Germany, Italy, Great Britain, France—only France, since 1945, has hesitated about her destiny.

Chancellor Adenauer has led his party and his country with un-bending determination, his eyes fixed on the goal: to inspire confidence in the new Germany, to ally the Federal Republic with the West with indestructible bonds, and to organize European unity through a reconciliation with France. A wise policy, but one imposed by circumstances, one may say: the Bonn government had no choice. The objection is not entirely valid; a fragment of a people and of a territory, the Germany of Bonn could have hesitated, following an old Germanic tradition, between "orientation toward the West" and "orientation toward the East": that is, under the new conditions, between the attempt at reunification by agreement with the Soviet Union, and European or Atlantic integration. She did not hesitate, thanks to the ascendancy of one man, the Chancellor, and of one party, the Christian Democrats.

Italy had many fewer motives for hesitation than West Germany. With a large Communist Party, the memory of an imperial enter-prise which had ended in disaster, and a large population on a narrow strip of land, she could not aspire to the role of a great power. No grandiose goal offered itself to an Italian nationalism. The accession to the rank of full membership in the Atlantic Alliance, of equal partnership in a united Europe, all seemed, in 1945, the honorable goals of a diplomacy suggested by events and consistent with wisdom.

Once the smoke of battle had cleared, Great Britain, like France, found herself in a world deeply transformed. Sir Winston Churchill had still declared, during the war, that he had not become His Majesty's Prime Minister to preside over the liquidation of the empire. The voters elected his rival, who solemnly promised, and granted according to his promises, the independence of India and Burma. The rest followed inevitably, first in Asia, then in the Near East. The evacuation of the Suez Canal Zone was a result of the independence of India, since the Indian army under British command had previously assumed the responsibility of defending the lines of communication between the mother country and its distant possessions. In spite of an impulse to the contrary in 1956, the political class of Great Britain consented almost unanimously, either with firmness or resignation, to liquidate the imperial possessions. England made every effort to keep the protectorates in the oil-bearing regions of the Near East as long as possible. In Africa, Conservatives and Labourites shared in the task of creating independent states in the west and multi-racial states in the east. The first formula was put into practice where there were no British settlements of great importance. In Kenya and Rhodesia the settlers were neither asked to leave nor authorized to take South Africa as an example.

England without her empire was no longer on the scale of the "Great Powers." In theory, she could have taken the lead in the movement for European unity and insisted on becoming the representative of the old Continent in the councils of the world. Almost unanimously she refused that new course, and chose a traditional diplomacy, modified to meet new conditions. Through the Atlantic Alliance and the German participation in the common defense, the equivalent of the European balance of power was restored; since a land power now dominated half of the old Continent, it was an

alliance, not rivalry, between Germany and France that would give
Great Britain security compatible with Russian hegemony and the
atomic age. Great Britain still was free, after the end of the colonial
era, to continue the activities which had led her, perhaps somewhat inadvertently, to control the largest, and one of the least
durable, empires that history has known. But commerce was no
longer to open the way for armies, cargoes were to do without the
protection of the Royal Navy, and influence was to take the place
of power.

France was in a unique position because she still had the interests
and obligations of a great power without the resources of one. In
order to carry on eight years of war in Indochina, she needed American aid. In order to transfer most of her army to Algeria she had to
leave to others the care of assuring her security. In certain respects
France, like Germany, Italy, and Great Britain, was compelled by
events: she could not refuse to cooperate with the countries of
Western Europe and the Atlantic Pact. But she was still free to
decide what form that cooperation would take, free to commit most
of her economic and military strength either in Europe or overseas.
Let us even ignore those who voted, consciously or not, for the Soviet
camp, or those who were hoping for a more independent diplomacy,
nationalist on the right, neutralist on the left: the partisans of the
Atlantic Alliance who governed France from 1946 to 1958 refused
to sacrifice either Asia to Africa, or Africa to Europe, or European
unity to the French Union. Each group gave intransigent expression
to its hopes or plans: the so-called European party *insisted* on a
federal union of the European Six with a transfer of sovereignty; the
anti-Europeans denounced supranational organizations as a betrayal
of "eternal France." No group exhibited the pragmatism which
would have made possible a course at once resolute and moderate.

The crisis of the regime came in 1958 during the "decolonization"
process, at a time when France was incapable of attaining either
of the goals she was stubbornly trying to attain simultaneously:
pacification in Algeria and the Common Market.

Is the "dictatorial" investiture of General de Gaulle intended to facilitate or delay French adjustment to the world and choice of policy? There is no answer so far. General de Gaulle is making every effort to find agreement with the Algerian nationalists and at the same time maintain a French Algeria. He promises to spend hundreds of billions of francs in North and Black Africa without giving up the development of the Common Market. He insists that France have equal rank with the United States and Great Britain in the triumvirate directing the Atlantic Alliance, and does not realize that European unification is incompatible with this world role. Like all the governments which came before him, he refuses to adjust French ambitions to the level of her resources. He dictates the goals in the expectation that "the Quartermaster Corps will follow."

Two courses are still open for France; the Europe of the Six is potentially a great power whose resources are not less than those of the continent-states. If France's overseas activities are not incompatible with Western ideals, if peace is restored in Algeria, the task of economic development with Eurafrica as a final result, which France cannot accomplish alone, could be considered as a common European responsibility.

If France refuses to commit herself fully to the Europe of the Six, if she insists on freedom of action in Africa, she can play an honorable part, but not that of a great power, in the Atlantic Alliance and world affairs.

For the time being General de Gaulle's policy is as uncertain as that of his predecessors: he refuses to make a choice. He commits himself to carry out the provisions of the treaty of Rome and solicits the support of Chancellor Adenauer against the British-inspired free-tariff area. But at the same time, contrary to the spirit of the treaty of Rome, he claims a place in the Council of the Great Powers. Algeria and the African Community are the responsibility of France alone, even though our allies have in the past made up the deficits in our foreign finances and are presently affected by the transfer of the French Army to Africa.

When men do not make up their minds, events decide for them.

The Fourth Republic was unable to achieve either the mutation of the empire or the unification of Europe, because it refused to sacrifice all or part of French sovereignty for the good of the peoples overseas or of our European partners. General de Gaulle is trying to avoid these sacrifices by pursuing a policy both nobler and better adapted to the times. But one man cannot change the world. Neither alone nor with Africa, which is for the time being a liability rather than an asset, can France attain first magnitude on a world scale. Committed to Europe, and Europe's agent in Africa, she might well claim a higher mission. Either way, she has an honorable future before her. But if she continues to arrogate to herself alone a role which can be assigned only to Europe, if she tries to keep for herself the advantages of both an independent diplomacy and European solidarity, she is once again running the risk of losing on both counts, and of again finding herself alone, not with her means increased to measure up with her ambitions, but with her interests reduced to the level of her means.

CONCLUSION

A people so constant in its fundamental impulses that we can still recognize it in portraits made of it two or three thousand years ago, and at the same time so changeable in its daily thoughts and tastes that it finally becomes an unanticipated spectacle even to itself; thus Frenchmen are often quite as startled as any foreigner at the things they have just done. Left to themselves they are the most home-loving and routine-bound of men, and yet, when torn unwillingly from home and habits, the French are willing to push to the ends of the earth and dare any-thing. The French are unruly by temperament, yet feel more comfortable under the arbitrary and even violent rule of an autocrat than under orderly and free government by their leading citizens. One moment the French are declared enemies of authority, and the next we find them submitting with a zeal such as peoples best fitted for servitude cannot attain. So long as no one resists, the French may be led on a thread, but they become ungovernable the moment the example of resistance is offered anywhere. Thus the French are always deceiving their masters, who fear them either too much or not enough, for they are never so free that the possibility of enslaving them must be ruled out, nor so subjugated that they may not still cast off the yoke. Fitted for all things, yet excelling only in war; preferring danger, violence, success, glamour, and fame to true glory; more capable of heroism than of virtue, of genius than of common sense; quick to conceive grandiose designs rather than to achieve great undertakings; the French constitute the most brilliant and the most dangerous nation in Europe, and the best qualified to become in turn an object of admiration, hatred, pity or terror,—but never of indifference.

If we leave out the phrase "fitted for all things but excelling only in war," this portrait of the French nation, steadfast and changing, presents a picture of striking and current truth. *The Old Regime and the French Revolution* appeared in 1856. A century later, a Socialist minister dispatched an expeditionary force to conquer the Suez Canal. Two years later, the French submitted to an "autocrat" with a unanimity and a "zeal for submission" that peoples "best fitted for servitude" might well envy. More republican than parliamentary, more Caesarean than monarchic, more agitated than dynamic, France in the twentieth century resembles the France of the last century and of always, unpredictable in her sudden reversals, constant in her fundamental impulses.

The "system" has vanished, the struggle for power is in abeyance, the parties are disqualified, and Gaullist conformism masks yesterday's quarrels, which will be those of tomorrow. The perennial call for a regrouping of parties runs into the same subtle and insurmountable obstacles. The new Constitution allows the government to dictate a policy which those elected by the people would be incapable of formulating and are reluctant to accept. As long as General de Gaulle is there and war in Algeria continues, the parties, discredited, and the professionals in Parliament, uncertain of their fate, will bow to the authority of an absolute, enlightened, and benevolent monarch. But nonhereditary monarchies are temporary expedients: a democracy becomes stable when obedience is given to institutions, not to individuals, and when a national crisis does not automatically endanger the constitution.

Some progress has been made since the last century. The legitimacy of democracy, in spite of the fuss aroused by the cliques of the extreme right, is no longer seriously debated. A military *coup d'état* might have succeeded in May 1958 because the French in Algeria had accidentally obtained the cooperation of the army. But the people, who would not have fought to save the Parliament, would soon have regretted the lost liberties. A representative form of government, with elections, parties, and an assembly, is the normal expression of French society in the twentieth century.

Why has this form of government been constantly threatened for the last thirty years? The threat, as we have seen, is created less by the enemies of the regime than by functional difficulties and national frustrations. The difficulties and frustrations lead us in turn to the economic substructure, to the influence of the past, to the historical conjuncture, and to the national character. The uncertainty arises in the question of the proper share to attribute to each of these causes.

In France, and even more outside France, one school of thought emphasizes the resistance of peasant proprietors, shopkeepers, and the heads of family enterprises to the industrial revolution. Because agriculture has been protected and precapitalist forms have survived, the rise in the standard of living has been slowed down, the workers, victims of agricultural and commercial conservatism, have isolated themselves in the consciousness of an oppressed class, expressing their hostility by voting against the State, which they label "bourgeois." This interpretation unquestionably expresses one aspect of the truth. But does it account for the electoral behavior of the French, the behavior of the politicians? I am not convinced of it. At any rate, the modernization of the economy now taking place constitutes a decisive test in this respect.

Meanwhile, it must be noted that the workers are not turned away from their pseudorevolutionary attitude by either high wages (by European standards) or good housing conditions. The institutional crisis in 1958 was neither provoked nor forestalled by the expansion of industry and an unprecedented prosperity. It is logical to think that growth of population and production will convert the next generation to a more rational attitude toward the State and the outer world. One cannot be sure, since the factionalism of today has its source in the contradictory responses to the problems which confronted the country.

In the last century it was tempting to blame incompatible traditions and the unending repetition of the same battles between the same groups, each the prisoner of an unshakable and sterile fidelity. There is nothing like this in our time. Because the Republic was unable to put an end to the economic crisis, or adopt a policy toward the Third Reich during the 1930's or prevent invasion and defeat in the forties or take the initiative in the mutation of the empire in the fifties, twice the parliamentarians have had to appeal to a savior.

Were the institutions responsible? Again I hesitate to answer: economic leaders had not understood the nature of the depression and the conditions for recovery any better than those in the government. Military leaders were not blameless for the army's lack of adaptation to mechanized warfare. Public opinion, and even more the politicians, did not appreciate the strength of Asian and African nationalism and the excessive cost of putting down rebellions. The first insurrections in Algeria (Sétif) and Morocco took place during the provisional government of General de Gaulle. He had appointed Admiral Thierry d'Argenlieu in Indochina and he, too, had in mind a compromise with the spirit of the times without the surrender of sovereignty.

It was, then, less the past than the present that weighed heavily on the last years of the Third Republic, and on the first years of the Fourth. France had to assume tasks which were beyond her strength. From this felt disproportion between obligations and means emerged a defeatism expressed by the alternation of contradictory attitudes. And, as usual, the nation showed its uncertainties in its passionate debates, in which considerations of expediency and invocations of principle mingled: Ethiopia, Munich, armistice, war in Indochina, E.D.C., war in Algeria; at each of these stages in their common history, Frenchmen were united only in accusing each other of treason and denying their faith.

If we look to the future, past the war in Algeria, past a decade of economic progress, we no longer see the principal causes of this crisis in France. Modernization has reached the whole of society; the standard of living is at least as high as in the most advanced European countries today; foreign obligations have been reduced to fit resources. Will France now have the same wisdom of purpose as Sweden or Great Britain? Will she prefer to build houses in Paris rather than ports in Africa and roads in the Sahara? I cannot refrain from repeating what Tocqueville wrote: "When torn unwillingly from home and habits, the French are willing to push to the ends of the earth—preferring danger, violence, success, glamour and fame." If France has had trouble adapting herself to the industrial and bourgeois civilization of the twentieth century, it is also because she had always, as a community, preferred power to business and the ideal to reasonable order.

All peoples, it is said, are captives of the most glorious period in their history. France would thus not succeed in escaping the memory of the Sun King or the image of the great nation spreading throughout Europe the new symbols of liberty, equality, and fraternity. Because she had perfected the national state, thanks to the joint achievements of the Monarchy and the Republic, she would cling today to anachronistic ideologies and would be incapable of meeting the challenge of the present.

The historical changes of our time, it is true, strike a blow at certain ideologies which have become an integral part of the French consciousness. Universality of civilization? Tunisians and Moroccans, Algerians, the very people who have assimilated our culture, all claim the right to become states for themselves and proclaim in turn the absolutism of sovereignty. National unity? The educational subject matter was the same throughout the territories over which the tricolor flew, and the elites of Vietnam or Africa received Western culture in our language. Administrative centralization? For a long time the French empire was subject to directives which came from Paris; today centralization is weakening before the demands of the Franco-African Community, European unity, and the renewed vitality of some provinces. Whether the whole is Europe, North Africa, or Black Africa, France can hardly play the part to which she aspires beyond her borders except by transcending the Jacobin heritage, the heritage of a nationalism that denies the *others* their individuality and diversity even within the nation itself.

Have the French refused to make this intellectual adjustment? The obstacles, I believe, have been in the facts as much as in the ideas. After all, the right of the peoples to dispose of themselves is also a French idea; although the Vietnamese or the Algerians were not allowed this right, the denial was in no way, even unconsciously, caused by the universality of French civilization. A part of French public opinion has been more passionately anticolonialist than its counterpart in England. Those who justified, if not those who directed, the war in Indochina and the pacification of Algeria invoked the danger of Communism, the oil of the Sahara, France's mission in Africa, and safeguarding the status of a great power. Finally, if some politicians repeated the formula of integration, put Algeria and Brittany on the same level, promised to treat the Arabs or the Kabyles as Parisians or Provençals, it was because in order to put principles into effective practice there was no other recourse but to "conceive grandiose designs": to change, in the middle of the twentieth century, nine million Moslems into Frenchmen—which surely bears witness to "more genius than common sense."

Would fifteen additional years of economic expansion, ten million more men, the break-up of the empire, and the unity of Europe be enough for the French to lose their "fundamental impulses" and stop being "recognizable in the portraits made of them" throughout the ages? Perhaps a transformation of the family structure and a radical educational reform would produce Frenchmen who would be less harshly judged by the liberals à la Tocqueville or the members of the labor parties across the Channel or Atlantic. But do critics either at home or abroad *really* with all their hearts want this conversion? The acceptance of industrial society, the gain in population and vitality, the end of the barren struggles against nationalisms— yes, these steps of the adjustment to the world were necessary and are now being taken. But must indices of production haunt Frenchmen's dreams, must colonies be abandoned because they cost too much, must business have preference over glory?

Would Tocqueville have wanted Frenchmen to be other than as he described them?

POSTSCRIPT

The Fifth Republic is completing its first year as I write this postscript. By the time this book appears, two years will have elapsed since the revolution of May 1958. Some new variations on the theme of "France, steadfast and changing" have become apparent.

On the surface, change is the dominant feature of constitutional and economic policies. The Constitution and the practice of the new regime differ from those of the Fourth Republic as much as one type of Western democracy can differ from another (the Fifth Republic, in fact, retains the fundamental characteristics of Western democracy: multiple parties, free elections, personal liberties). From 1953 to 1957, the keynote was one of expansion: to it, those in power blithely sacrificed price stability and the reserves of foreign exchange. Measures taken since the end of 1958 have strengthened the currency and permitted the freeing of exchange rates. Those now in power have agreed to slacken the rate of expansion to ensure the equilibrium of the balance of payments.

On the other hand, continuity seems to characterize policy toward Black Africa and Algeria. The *loi-cadre* of M. Gaston Defferre led to the Community of 1958 and this, in turn, led to the independence of the Mali Federation. Neither public opinion nor the politicians has been violently opposed to the "decolonization" of the French territories south of the Sahara. Similarly, the offer made by General de Gaulle to Algeria, for self-determination in the four years following a cease-fire or the completion of pacification, resembles the three-point plan of M. Guy Mollet (cease-fire, elections, negotiations). The formula for self-determination is better than that for elections. The result would be equivalent in either case, if circumstances permitted putting them into practice.

Finally, the foreign policy of General de Gaulle resembles that of his predecessors on the very points where one expected (with hope or with dread) the greatest number of changes: Michel Debré has promised to respect strictly the letter and the spirit of the Treaty of Rome that he had passionately attacked. In the framework of the Atlantic Alliance, however, a framework which he does not question, the President of the Republic rejects military "integration." The style of Gaullist diplomacy is certainly completely different from that of the Fourth Republic. In what way is its content revolutionary? Frenchmen and foreigners still wonder.

The following pages will show, I hope, that permanence and change, continuity and reversals, blend in a subtle and sometimes paradoxical fashion within each of these spheres. The France of the Fifth Republic deceives those who love simple ideas just as much as did the France of the Fourth Republic.

*   *   *

The French have done much voting since the May 1958 revolution: constitutional referendum, legislative elections, election of the President of the Republic, municipal elections and senatorial elections. All the institutions provided for in the Constitution, from the highest to the lowest, have been established or re-established.

Among these elections three reflect the sharp change which took place in 1958 and two indicate the continuity (one could almost say the constancy) of the political life of the country. When the question arose of approving or disapproving the Constitution, 79.25 per cent of the voters answered *oui*. Of course, this *oui* was meant for a man, rather than for a text which is complex and, for the average citizen, obscure. But the fact remains: the confidence of the French in a man led them to support the Constitution which this man proposed to them.

The same transference of confidence manifested itself in the legislative elections, although less strongly. The party which explicitly identified itself with General de Gaulle, which had no other program but one of supporting the acts of the General, the Union for the New Republic (U.N.R.) was the greatest victor. Made up for the most part of former members of the R.P.F., it succeeded in electing more than 200 deputies out of 540 on the second ballot. But the electoral system (single-member constituencies with election by majority on the first ballot, or plurality on the second) had greatly favored it: on the first ballot, its candidates received fewer votes (17.6 per cent) than the candidates of the Communist Party (18.9 per cent), but, because of withdrawals before the second ballot, more than 200 U.N.R. deputies were ultimately elected. As a result of the electoral law, the representation of the extreme parties, the Communists and the Poujadists (which the backers of the electoral law had hoped to reduce), was almost completely eliminated: there are no longer any Poujadists at all in the Palais-Bourbon and but ten Communists. By voting for the U.N.R. (frequently represented by an almost unknown candidate), the voters thought rightly or wrongly that they were voting for the General himself. As for him, he received 78.5 per cent of the votes of the presidential electors at at the end of the year.

The popularity of the Chief of State, on the other hand, had no visible effect on the municipal or senatorial elections. The U.N.R., encouraged by its recent and unforeseen success, hoped to obtain control of numerous municipalities, especially those held by the Communists, as well as those held by the politicians of the Fourth Republic. The U.N.R.'s assault broke against the electoral conservatism of the country.

Contrary to party directives, more than a quarter of the Communist voters must have answered *oui* in the referendum. Many of these dissidents had voted for the U.N.R. candidates in the legislative elections. In the municipal elections, the Communist Party regained its former strength, and although the change in the electoral law (from proportional representation to majority rule) caused it to lose a few municipalities, it retained most of those it held, and because of the electoral law it now holds them alone (where it obtained a plurality of votes on the second ballot, the entire Communist slate was elected).

As was to be expected, the senatorial elections confirmed the results of the municipal elections (the Senators are elected by an electoral college dominated by municipal councillors). The traditional parties are strongly represented in the new Senate,[1] whereas the U.N.R. is only a minority group of forty-four senators. The leading politicians of the Fourth Republic (Gaston Defferre, Edgar Faure) who had been defeated in the legislative elections reappeared in the Senate. The first ebb of the Gaullist tide laid bare a political pattern which had been hardly changed.

The situation created by these elections, some of them Gaullist, the others traditional, differs fundamentally from that foreseen by either supporters or critics of the Constitution. The latter considered the limitations on the powers of the Assembly elected by universal suffrage to be exaggerated, the prerogatives of the Senate to be excessive, and the powers of a President of the Republic elected for seven years to be disproportionate. But the U.N.R. group controls an absolute majority in the National Assembly with the support of the 71 Algerian deputies. The opponents of the Constitution came for the most part from the left, from the extreme left, or from liberals in the Tocqueville tradition. All of them, regardless of their origin, felt more distant from the National Assembly majority composed of Algerian and U.N.R. deputies than they did from General de Gaulle himself. As a result, by a new paradox, those who are theoretically hostile to the power of the Chief of State rejoice when General de Gaulle uses and abuses the authority given him by the Constitution; those who are theoretically favorable to a reduction in the powers of the National Assembly deplore the fact that the parliamentary majority dedicated to the defense of French Algeria is held in check by the all-powerful resident of the Elysée Palace.

---

[1] 74 Independents, 20 Peasants, 34 Popular Republicans, 51 Socialists, 14 Communists, and 64 deputies of the Democratic Left.

Such a situation—the monarch more liberal than the majority of deputies elected in his name—is not without precedent: Louis XVIII was more moderate than the *Chambre introuvable,* but the latter had been elected by limited suffrage, whereas the current Assembly was elected by universal suffrage.

Circumstances, then, do not yet permit us to judge the Fifth Republic. In one sense, one is tempted to say that the 1958 Constitution has not yet been tested. The current regime is fundamentally "Gaullist"; it constitutes the transition between the Fourth and the Fifth Republic, and it is the regime of a savior acclaimed by almost the entire nation in the hope that he may find a solution to apparently insoluble problems.

Between yesterday and today the contrast is striking. Yesterday, the government was supposed to reflect in its very make-up the shades of parliamentary opinion; the game of politics was continuous, the existence of the Cabinet was threatened at each moment. Today, the President of the Republic, invested with supreme power, is elected for seven years; the ministers, though theoretically responsible to the Assembly, are the interpreters and executive agents of the Chief of State rather than the representatives of the parliamentary majority. President de Gaulle's power is, in fact, if not according to the letter of the Constitution, greater than that of the American President, for the latter must obtain the approval of both houses of Congress for many of his decisions, whereas the French President, because of the expedient of semifictitious ministerial responsibility, escapes that necessity.

But this situation is due rather to the facts than to the texts. Nothing in the text of the Constitution authorizes the President of the Republic to offer the right of self-determination to peoples inhabiting a part of the national territory whose integrity was solemnly restated by the Constitution. Nothing in the text justifies the formula used by the President of the National Assembly of the "preserves of the Chief of State" (diplomacy, army, Algeria). The text is ambiguous on the essential points of the division of power between the President of the Republic and the Prime Minister, but it is the personality of General de Gaulle, and the loyalty of Michel Debré which are responsible for the current division: the President of the Republic makes the great decisions, and the Prime Minister manages daily affairs.

The Constitution could likewise eventually provoke conflicts between the executive and the legislature, but these conflicts, currently latent, cannot have serious consequences because of the composition of the majority. Of the 200 U.N.R. deputies, how many would be re-elected if the Chief of State repudiated them and dissolved the Assembly? The Assembly complains that it is not treated with enough respect by the ministers. The spirit of rivalry and almost of hostility between executive and legislative, a characteristic element of French political history, was immediately revived by a Constitution which attempts to establish by law the supremacy of the government over the Assembly—a supremacy created in Great Britain by the discipline of the majority party. Whatever one's personal preferences, no one can appraise the value of the "new system" so long as the parliamentary majority cannot revolt because it would inevitably be defeated in a test of strength with the President of the Republic.

Future constitutional practice is uncertain. It is no easier to foresee what the parties will look like after the ebb of the Gaullist wave. The 1956 Assembly was ungovernable for lack of a majority; the 1958 Assembly is too easily manipulated for lack of an opposition, or at least of an open opposition. Yesterday instability was feared, today an excessive rigidity on the part of institutions and men is dreaded. On one fundamental point, however, French politics have remained the same, faithful to their reputation for paradox: the Algerian policy of the Chief of State corresponds more closely to the preferences of those who oppose it than to the secret desires of those who approve it.

*   *   *

As I have tried to indicate in this book, the French economy has made remarkable progress since the war. The index of industrial production reached 160 in the spring of 1958 (on the basis of 100 in 1952). Since industrial manpower hardly increased, the rise in production reflected an increased productivity, which, in the years 1954–1956, was of the order of 6 to 8 per cent a year. These results were jeopardized by an inflationary push which, beginning in 1956, led to considerable deficits in the balance of payments. In 1956 and 1957 the Fund for the Stabilization of Exchange Rates lost more than a billion dollars yearly. At the end of 1957, France had to borrow half a billion dollars from the O.E.E.C. and the United States. Severe measures were taken at the end of 1957 (restrictive credit policies, "ordinary" budget—"above the line," in the British expression—showing a surplus), which began to take effect in the spring of 1958 just when the political crisis led first to a flight of capital and then, after the creation of the de Gaulle government, to a return of capital. The loan floated by Antoine Pinay permitted the Fund to recover a hundred and fifty to two hundred million dollars in gold. By the end of the year prices were generally stabilized and exports (f.o.b.) covered more than 90 per cent of the imports (c.i.f.), which implies a state of equilibrium in the balance of trade. At this point, in the last days of December 1958 the government promulgated by decree the 1958 budget, which, together with the devaluation of the franc, was considered the beginning of a new policy.

This policy, which is far less doctrinaire than has been claimed, was dictated by considerations of expediency and put certain classical procedures into effect. In brief it was a combination of three actions: *anti-inflationary measures* (credit restriction and "ordinary" budget surplus, thanks to cuts in subsidies and the adoption of supplementary taxes), *devaluation* to favor exports and check imports, and *liberalization of trade* to meet the requirements of the O.E.E.C. and the Common Market. Credit restrictions and the freeing of exchange rates were to limit price increases which the devaluation and the discontinuance of subsidies tended to provoke.

This *blueprint for financial and economic soundness* had been recommended by the committee of experts headed by Jacques Rueff. It is certainly liberal, but it is no more liberal than the policy adopted by all the other countries of western Europe. It indicates France's adjustment to circumstances, and the acceptance of rules already put into practice by our neighbors and partners in the Common Market.

The new policy has been a complete success. The movement of capital has been reversed. The Fund for the Stabilization of Exchange Rates has recovered in a year between a billion and a half and two billion dollars. At the end of 1958, France's short-term obligations exceeded gold and foreign-exchange reserves by more than half a billion dollars; at the end of 1959, there was nearly a billion dollars to spare. The balance of trade has produced a surplus every month for the past six months.

The rise in prices which the devaluation of the franc and the discontinuance of subsidies rendered inevitable has not surpassed 5 to 6 per cent and has remained within the range predicted by the experts. The social difficulties feared by some have failed to materialize. Nor has there been a crisis or increased unemployment. The level of production has remained high. The index of industrial production, corrected for seasonal variations, was at 165 in October 1959, compared to 156 in May 1958 and 151 in January 1959. Although growth slackened with respect to previous years, it has nonetheless picked up once again.

Is there a relationship between the Fifth Republic and the new economic policy, between Gaullism and a more liberal method? Let us be quite frank; the relationship is in large part accidental. The Minister of Finance hesitated to take certain rigorous measures recommended to him by the experts. Some spokesmen of the U.N.R. were more interested in expansion than in monetary stability. The choice was partly determined by circumstances: the lack of reserves of foreign exchange and the need for free exchange rates when the Common Market was established definitely required a policy of financial orthodoxy whose two major elements were a tight budget and the devaluation of the franc. How could France alone in western Europe reject the convertibility of currency and how could she have risked such an experiment without putting an end to inflation? The merit of the experts in having conceived, and that of General de Gaulle in having adopted, the series of measures taken in December 1958 is not diminished for these reasons.

Let us add that the spectacular success that so many Frenchmen misunderstand as yesterday they misunderstood the exchange crisis, the success that has restored foreign respect for the French currency, would not have been possible had not the economy at the end of the Fourth Republic been healthier and more vigorous in depth than superficial observers believed. The optimistic judgment that I made in October 1957 at Harvard and which is repeated in Chapter III of this book tends today to be ratified by the majority of the experts. It is true that all the dangers have not miraculously disappeared. It remains to be seen what the rate of growth of production will be during a period of monetary stability. The obligations of the country in Algeria, in the African territories south of the Sahara, and at home remain heavy. It will require some years yet before the more numerous generations enter the labor market.

In spite of everything, of all the countries of western Europe, France holds the best cards, on paper. After a long period of decline or stagnation, the population is on the increase. The proportion of young people is growing. Those under fifteen years old in France make up 24.5 per cent of the population, in Western Germany 21.5 per cent. In absolute figures, they are more numerous in France than in the Federal Republic. The modernization of agriculture frees a labor force which will be more productive in industry. The retarded sectors or enterprises will in their turn be swept along by the movement of rationalization. If the French were to be concerned only with themselves and their own well-being, the road of the future would be open straight before them.

*   *   *

The Community appeared to many observers as the most interesting innovation of the Constitution. Between the maintenance of the status of the colonies, an impossibility in the long run, and the multiplication of states juridically independent but lacking the resources necessary to the effective exercise of sovereignty, did not the Community offer an intermediate path?

With respect to international law, the Community is poorly defined and does not fall into any of the classic categories. Were it a federation, the French Republic would no longer exist and would be no more than one of the federated republics, just as California and Texas are states belonging to the United States of America. Were it a confederation, all the African republics—Madagascar, Congo, or Senegal—would have a flag, an army, ambassadors, representatives in the U.N. Neither one of these typical formulas translates the political or legal reality of the Community.

With respect to international law, the republics of the Community still belong essentially to the zone of French sovereignty; they do not have the attributes of external sovereignty. The President of the French Republic is the President of the Community. The ministers for affairs common to both France and the Community are the French ministers for the appropriate departments (foreign affairs, finance, national education, and so on). General de Gaulle, however, has chosen four ministers from among the African politicians as counselors to the Community. Some republics will be represented in international organizations. The Republic of Madagascar has some of the attributes of external sovereignty.

But perhaps we should put these statements in the past tense, because the Community in the form in which it was conceived and realized in 1958 has probably already ceased to exist. In accepting in Saint-Louis and Dakar that the Mali Federation could become independent without leaving the Community, General de Gaulle has given up the alternatives of *Community* or *secession,* and has accepted a third possibility: an *independence* which would not be secession; at the same time, the movement of all the African republics toward independence or external sovereignty seems irresistible.

In 1958, when the new Constitution was drawn up, three schools of thought could be discerned among African political leaders. The first, that of Sékou Touré, favored immediate and total independence; the second, that of the *Parti du Regroupement Africain* (P.R.A.) temporarily supported the Community, but with the hope of forcing a regrouping into "primary federations" of the African republics too small to constitute truly independent states, and with a commonwealth or a confederation of sovereign states as the final objective; a third school of thought, that of Félix Houphouët-Boigny, supported the Community, not with the purpose of leaving it, but to remain in it as the Community evolved toward an authentic federation.

In the referendum, the first school of thought triumphed only in Guinea, which became independent. During 1959 Senegal and Sudan united in a primary federation, called the Mali Federation, and the leaders of this federation communicated to Paris their desire to obtain independence in accord with France and without breaking with the Community. The problem posed by Sékou Touré and Guinea was presented a second time, but with consequences which were this time irreparable.

General de Gaulle could answer a second time that independence was equivalent to secession and that it could only be an expression of hostility toward France. In this case, the Community, dismantled by the secession of Guinea and the Mali Federation, would run the risk of going to pieces, Black Africa would dissolve into sovereign states forced to a position of hostility toward France because of the conditions under which they received independence. Or else General de Gaulle could use the article of the Constitution relating to agreements of association and could attempt to reduce the differences between the states belonging to the Community and the independent states tied to the Community by agreements of association. In this case, however, all the states would tend to demand independence, at least in the form of the attributes of external sovereignty (embassies, representation in the U.N.). General de Gaulle very wisely chose the second alternative. He did not oppose the independence of the Mali Federation. The die is cast; the number of completely independent African states will rapidly increase. British Nigeria, French Togoland, and Cameroons, as well as the Mali Federation, will become independent in 1960. It is likely that the states that are more loyal to the Community will also follow the same path. The ideology of total independence triumphs over all arguments, even those of wisdom.

The outcome, we must admit, is a logical one. The Community in the form in which it was established in 1958 did not bring about equality between the French Republic and the African Republics. Legal equality between the partners of the Community would have required a federation or a confederation, in other words, either equality among all the individual citizens of the Community, or among the states. But in the case of a federation, France also would have had to undergo a truly revolutionary mutation and grant legislative sovereignty to the Community Assembly, and the right to adopt taxes which some would have had to pay and whose benefits would have been in part distributed to others. The federation in fact was not feasible; as a result, a confederation was both the rational and probable outcome. One may even hope that the intellectual, economic, and even political bonds that the Community was to consolidate will for the most part survive the establishment of independent African states.

Let us delay a moment to remember the events of the thirteenth of May. Those who conspired against the Fourth Republic and who finally toppled it denounced the "auctioneers of the empire." They brought about the establishment of the Fifth Republic, which, in the African territories south of the Sahara, accomplished faster and better what the previous regime had hoped but had not had the strength to do. The conspirators made possible what they wanted to prevent. A new twist of the cunning of reason, a disciple of Hegel would say: human passions serve objectives they ignore. A paradox of French politics, answers the historian; it takes the man who embodies French nationalism to "abandon" the empire without the public experiencing a sense of defeat or humiliation. Would the history of the Fourth Republic have been different had the head of the Rally of the French People spoken with the language of today's President of the Republic?

One cannot help but ask the same question about Algerian policy. One of my friends, who enjoys paradoxes, told me a few days after the thirteenth of May: "This is the beginning of Algerian independence." His words seemed a joke at the time. Less than two years later, the joke begins to be taken seriously. Certainly, if I stick to the facts, as I write General de Gaulle has not restored peace in Algeria and the increased attempts to put an end to the struggle without negotiations with the F.L.N. have all failed. To negotiate with the F.L.N. is in effect to recognize it as the representative of the Algerian people, and so to prejudge the result of the popular referendum. If the F.L.N. in fact represents the Algerian people, then the Algerians must want independence. This is not, moreover, merely an argument in logic. Should the F.L.N. participate in the administration of Algeria it would drive out the moderates with its revolutionary dynamism; total independence would be the inevitable outcome. For the "negotiations" with the F.L.N. not to be in themselves a triumph of the F.L.N., they would have to deal only with a cease-fire. If the nationalists break off the armed combat without having received recognition as representatives of the Algerian nation, without the political future of Algeria having been fixed, then a strictly military negotiation would not be the equivalent of a rebel victory. So the latter have consistently rejected the offer made first by Guy Mollet and then by General de Gaulle of a cease-fire not accompanied by a political agreement.

The last offer of the President of the Republic, the solemn proclamation of the right to self-determination—that is to say, of the right to independence—does not decisively alter the nature of the problem. How can the F.L.N. accept the cessation of armed hostilities without having obtained any guarantee other than the word of a man and the promise of a referendum in the four years following the end of hostilities? But, on the other hand, how could General de Gaulle, without sacrificing his own doctrine, without arousing the ire of his followers, give the F.L.N. more than he already has: that is to say, the right for all Algerians to choose their fate in a free election?

Practically speaking, the application of the principle of self-determination involves enormous difficulties in a country torn apart by war between a regular army and a guerrilla army. Who will insure the safety of the voters? If the regular army—the French army, of course—does so, the election would not be free in the eyes of the nationalists. Or the underground army could do so, but in this case the election would not be free in the eyes of the French. Is there a third alternative? This is not at all certain, because no military force outside of the French Army, even an international one, would be capable of preventing the underground army of the F.L.N. from organizing the population and dictating its vote.

If this analysis is correct, the conflict can prolong itself, and the only outcome would be either a total victory of the French army over the rebels (an improbable eventuality), or a secret agreement between the French government and the F.L.N. on a compromise solution that the two parties would commit themselves to respect for a number of years.

Whatever the judgment one makes on the Algerian problem—and the problem is one which may well have changed between the moment in which I write and that when this book will be offered to the reader—it is difficult to mistake the sense of evolution. By retaining the single electoral college—in other words, the political equality of all Algerians, both French and Moslem, conquerors and conquered—by recognizing solemnly the right of self-determination, General de Gaulle has practically accepted the independence of Algeria at an as yet undetermined date. Whatever the advantages of an association with France, the Algerian masses, caught between independent Tunisia and Morocco, will not resist the current which carries with it today an entire continent toward what appears to its inhabitants to be emancipation.

Although the final outcome is not in doubt, the terms and the date remain so. Algiers and Oran are French cities; the petroleum of the Sahara has been discovered and developed by French capital and technology. General de Gaulle cannot and does not want to abandon these French assets to the discretion of the F.L.N. Should the F.L.N. continue to be intransigent, a compromise could perhaps be attempted in the form of a partition similar to that of Palestine or Ireland. The partition itself would be a misfortune for everyone and the origin of new conflicts.

As long as the war in Algeria goes on, the destiny of the Fifth Republic will remain unpredictable. The events at the end of January, which went to the brink of tragedy, are enough to remind us of this fundamental fact.

The conspiracy organized by the Algerian "Ultras" has been a failure, in the end, and its leaders are today in prison. Faced with the clear necessity of a choice between an open *coup d'état* and discipline, the leaders of the army decided to follow the orders of the Chief of State. But it remains that a fraction of the officer corps did sympathize with the insurrection, that the authority of General de Gaulle was publicly challenged for many days. After the crisis, the institutions of the Fifth Republic looked more precarious than ever. The President stood firm; the State was weak.

In spite of economic progress, France is still in a half-revolutionary crisis without an accepted regime. Everything depends on one man— one man, alone and solitary. And nobody knows if even this man, in spite of his unique prestige, is able to impose an Algerian policy of peace upon the French army.

*   *   *

The leader of Fighting France and of the Provincial Government was remembered in Great Britain and the United States as a difficult partner. The President of the Fifth Republic has refreshed these memories and confirmed his reputation. But before considering the changes that General de Gaulle has introduced in the conduct of diplomacy, let us first consider, once again, the continuity. Most of those who appeal to General de Gaulle had violently opposed the E.D.C., then Euratom and the Treaty of Rome. The General himself had been hostile to the London agreements which in 1948 prepared the way for the creation of the Federal Republic, and he had publicly taken a position against the E.D.C. at a time when he was apparently retired from politics at Colombey-les-Deux-Eglises. Neither the Prime Minister nor the President of the Republic reopened the question of the Treaty of Rome. Even more, thanks to her strengthened financial position, the France of the Fifth Republic has been able to participate fully in the establishment of the Common Market —something the France of the Fourth Republic would have liked to do without perhaps having the capacity to do it.

General de Gaulle has likewise failed to indicate the slightest desire to "throw over the alliances" or even of "balancing" between East and West; he has deceived those who in the East counted on him to dissolve the Atlantic Alliance just as he has proven wrong those who in the West doubted his loyalty to the West. In the Berlin affair, he adopted the firmest attitude, partly to indicate his solidarity with Chancellor Adenauer and partly also because of his sincere conviction of the importance of the stakes.

In spite of everything, at the beginning of 1960, General de Gaulle is considered "a difficult partner" and some speak openly of a crisis in the Atlantic Alliance. What are the causes and the stakes of this crisis? If one attempts to grasp the essential features, beyond the routine incidents which will be forgotten in a few weeks or a few months, one perceives two characteristics of Gaullist policy which indicate if not a rupture at least a certain originality in relation to the preceding regime and which surprise, antagonize, and irritate our allies: the first is the drive for a truly French policy on an international level, a drive which renders more difficult the common diplomatic front of the West and prevents "military integration";

the second is the determination to extend the zone where French foreign policy is exercised and to obtain recognition, within the Atlantic Alliance, of a more glorious role for France than the one she has held for the past fifteen years. Diplomatic autonomy for a France restored to its rank of a power with world responsibility—such is the national ambition with which General de Gaulle wants to inspire France.

With this as a starting point, everything becomes easily understandable and the so-called paradoxes disappear. The Fifth Republic implements the Treaty of Rome, but the Europe of the Six is called *"l'Europe des patries";* national sovereignty is an absolute and transferrals of sovereignty to a supranational organism are condemned. The same desire for national autonomy is expressed in the refusal to stock atomic warheads in France (which led to the departure of 200 American medium-range bombers, previously stationed in France, for the Federal Republic and Great Britain), in the refusal to integrate the fighter squadrons, in the project to manufacture French atomic bombs and the establishment of a "striking force" under the sole orders of the French government. As to the desire to increase the role granted France, it has been expressed in the memorandum of September 1958, in the request for a three-nation directorate which would control the policies of the Atlantic Alliance throughout the world.

The so-called Gaullist policy of grandeur has a bad reputation outside France, both among our partners of the Six and among our Atlantic allies. To the drive for diplomatic autonomy is opposed the modern law of large groups of nations, the technical necessities of integration on the military level (in Europe, unintegrated fighter planes are incapable of fulfilling their mission), the disproportionate cost of atomic bombs and, even more, of the means of delivery. No one accepts the three-nation council beyond the degree of consultation which was the rule before the 1956 Suez expedition. In a general sense one criticizes Gaullist France for misunderstanding power relationships, for forgetting that the French Army, which is almost entirely in Algeria, is absent from Europe, for demanding a role which would be justified only once General de Gaulle had obtained his objectives (peace in Algeria, a regrouping around France of her former overseas possessions, and European organization). I will not deny the partial truth contained in these criticisms, especially since many of them are made in this book. General de Gaulle would be wrong to believe that France is not subject to the law of power which governs every foreign policy. He would be wrong to forget that the Bonn Republic, even while the most pro-French of Chancellors, Dr. Adenauer, is in power, no matter how faithful to the Common Market and the Europe of the Six, will oppose any French policy which would run the risk of weakening the Atlantic Alliance, which is considered the supreme guarantee.

But nothing allows us to affirm that the President of the Republic neglects these facts of the international situation. And on the other hand, our American friends would be wrong to misunderstand the changes that have taken place in the last ten years.

The United States is and will remain the leading country of the West. It alone possesses the economic resources and the technical capacity indispensable to military power in the atomic age. But undisputed leadership is no longer and can no longer be what it was yesterday. The monopoly or the unquestionable superiority of the United States in nuclear weapons and means of delivery has been replaced by equality, stalemate, and the equilibrium of terror. The European economies have recovered and have had for the past ten years a rate of growth higher than that of the American economy. The deficit in the American balance of payments indicates that between the Old and the New World there is no longer the dependence of one on the other but a reciprocal solidarity. As a result, even if the current claims of France are premature and excessive, one day or another Europe, and especially western Europe, will demand a more active role and a greater autonomy.

Gaullist France resembles the France of the Fourth Republic in that she has probably not chosen between two alternatives, that of a "united Europe" which would be a great power and that of traditional France, which, even with her internal affairs straightened out, even surrounded by her now independent former possessions and her European allies, can occupy an honorable but not a first-rank place on the world scene. In its profound uncertainty, the Fifth Republic resembles that which preceded it, in spite of a wholly external assurance and of grandiose declarations.

It would be no less dangerous to misunderstand the new realities which the President of the French Republic is interpreting in his personal style. Continental Europe is out of the dark; it has rebuilt its ruins and gives all signs of a renewed vitality. Perhaps the "policy of grandeur" contains in part an anachronism, perhaps it illustrates once again the love of "glamour and fame" of which Tocqueville speaks. It indicates also that the postwar period is coming to a close and that a new era is beginning in which neither France nor Europe will be content any longer to be objects of history.

INDEX

INDEX